Domestic Violence: Effectiveness of Intervention Programs

Gender Equality, Volume 4

Dr. Milos Kankaras

Published by Dr. Miloš Kankaraš, 2022.

While every precaution has been taken in the preparation of this book, the publisher assumes no responsibility for errors or omissions, or for damages resulting from the use of the information contained herein.

DOMESTIC VIOLENCE: EFFECTIVENESS OF INTERVENTION PROGRAMS

First edition. July 26, 2022.

ISBN: 979-8223969631

Written by Dr. Milos Kankaras.

Domestic Violence: Effectiveness of Intervention Programs

Dr Miloš Kankaraš

Executive summary

Domestic violence (DV) is a widespread form of abuse worldwide. Globally, the victims of domestic violence are overwhelmingly women, and women tend to experience more severe forms of violence. It is assumed that domestic violence is one of the most underreported crimes for both women and men. Over a quarter of married/partnered women aged 15 years or older have been subjected to physical and/or sexual violence from a current or former husband or intimate male partner at least once in their lifetime (WHO, 2018). Likewise, it is estimated that elder abuse affects almost one in six (more than 140 million) older people. There is a strong relationship between the level of gender equality in a given country and the incidence of domestic violence in the country, with less domestic violence occurring in countries with a higher level of gender equality.

Domestic violence was a long-overlooked and ignored policy issue despite its high prevalence. However, in recent decades, increased attention has been placed on various forms of domestic violence, including its most prevalent forms of intimate partner violence (IPV) and child abuse. The expanded policy focus has led to the global growth of the domestic violence intervention programmes of various forms, scopes and target types of violence.

However, as discussed in Landscaping Report 1 (Gender Equality: Frameworks, Actors and Available Empirical Evidence), the widest data gap exists where it matters the most – in measuring the impact of administered policy interventions. This is why in this report, we aim to present and evaluate existing empirical evidence on the effectiveness of interventions in the field of domestic violence gathered around the world so far. In other words, we will try to answer "what works", i.e., what is known to be an effective intervention strategy, under which conditions, and for which outcomes. Such evidence could then be used in designing future domestic violence interventions by avoiding identified inefficiencies and building upon observed effective aspects of these programmes.

The report is based on the literature review and summarises the findings presented in various systematic reviews and meta-analyses published over the last decade. We prioritised compiling evidence from rigorous empirical studies using experimental (i.e. randomised controlled trials – RCTs) and quasi-experimental designs. The evidence comprises studies on intimate partner violence, child abuse and maltreatment (including harmful traditional practices), child sexual abuse and elderly abuse. Other types of domestic abuse, such as abuse of pregnant women or abuse of persons with disabilities, are also reviewed where evidence is available. In the first chapter, we shortly discuss various forms of domestic and family violence, their prevalence, and their consequences. In chapter two, we outline some of the critical characteristics of domestic violence interventions and their incidence. Main empirical findings on the effectiveness of domestic violence interventions are discussed in chapter three, followed by the evaluation of limitations and gaps in presented evidence in chapter four.

Main findings

Strong growth of domestic violence intervention programmes during the last decade

Programmes aiming to prevent domestic violence started in the late 20th century and rapidly evolved during the last decade. At the same time, an increasing number of these interventions have applied elaborate impact assessments, thus slowly building up the evidence database on their effectiveness.

The large diversity of forms of domestic violence interventions

A variety of approaches have been used in domestic violence interventions. They differ across the type of violence they are focused on, the population group they target, the intervention strategy, the moment of intervention (i.e., primary vs secondary interventions), the location and geographical scope of the intervention (e.g., high-income vs LMIC contexts), etc. Domestic violence interventions are focused at the individual, group, community or system-wide levels. Common forms across these levels are one-on-one individual therapy or training sessions, work with couples and families, group-based training, community mobilisation efforts, or "gender transformative" programmes that aim to change system-wide settings. Most domestic violence interventions focus on primary or secondary prevention of IPV. But an increasing number of them are expanding their focus to the other forms of domestic violence. In particular, there is a small but growing number of programmes on domestic child abuse, elderly abuse, parental abuse, home care abuse, abuse of persons with disabilities, abuse of pregnant women, abuse of LGBTI+ persons, etc.

Three groups of sources of evidence on domestic violence intervention effectiveness

The domestic violence interventions' growth and effectiveness necessitated compiling systematic reviews of available empirical evidence in this area. Over the recent years, several systematic overviews of such empirical evidence have been published, although none of them is exclusively and comprehensively focused on all forms of domestic violence. Furthermore, most of the available reviews focus on specific domains of evidence, either in terms of geographic regions, particular intervention strategies or particular forms of domestic violence. In general, we can divide the available literature on the effectiveness of domestic violence intervention programmes into three groups. The first group of comprehensive reviews tackle all forms of violence against women and girls globally. Four such systematic reviews have been published in the last few years. The second group of sources consists of systematic reviews focused exclusively on particular forms of domestic violence, including individual reviews on IPV interventions, child abuse and elderly abuse. Finally, the third group of reviews consisted of meta-analyses focused on particular domestic violence intervention approaches or target populations. These include, for example, meta-analyses of the effectiveness of the interventions on perpetrators of IPV, reviews of the impact of advocacy interventions against various forms of VAWG, or systematic reviews of interventions preventing domestic violence against pregnant women.

A limited quantity of available empirical evidence on the effectiveness of domestic violence interventions

Maybe as a consequence of the intrinsic difficulty of the research topic, there is, in general, relatively little solid empirical evidence on the effectiveness of domestic violence intervention programmes. Moreover, there are entire domains of domestic violence (e.g., violence towards the elderly, against the parents, or persons with disabilities) that are researched with only a few evaluation studies. That has led most authors of systematic reviews and meta-analyses to resort to qualitative "narrative summaries" of the available evidence on programme effectiveness rather than more robust quantitative meta-analytic techniques. However, the scarcity of solid empirical evidence is not only due to the overall lack of domestic violence interventions. It is even more so to the lack of robust impact assessment studies in the applied interventions. In fact, in most systematic reviews, the number of intervention programmes with solid evaluation designs was a small fraction of all domestic violence interventions.

Positive change is possible

Examination of available empirical evidence shows that the desired reduction of incidences of various forms of domestic violence across different settings and situations is possible. Indeed, several domestic violence programmes have established empirical proof of the positive effects of their interventions.

<u>*High-income countries*</u>

Some primary prevention programmes have significantly reduced domestic violence incidence rates in high-income countries. For example, an intervention conducted in four family-planning clinics in Northern California found a 71% decrease in the odds of pregnancy coercion among women in the intervention group compared to participants in the control clinics. Likewise, two Canadian programmes on "Healthy Relationships" (Wolfe et al., 2009) showed significant reductions in dating violence perpetration in the intervention group compared to the control groups.

In the case of child abuse interventions in the high-income contexts, the effective interventions focused on increasing parents' self-confidence and were delivered by professionals only. Effect sizes of preventive interventions increased as follow-up duration increased, possibly indicating the so-called "sleeper effect"(i.e. a delayed impact on the programme recipient) of such interventions. For curative interventions, larger effect sizes were found for interventions focusing on improving parenting skills and those providing social or emotional support. The secondary interventions in the high-income countries with the victims of domestic violence have often shown success in enhancing survivors' physical and mental health. On the other hand, secondary prevention programmes with the perpetrators of IPV still offer limited effectiveness in reducing the rates of re-victimisation. There is also relatively limited success in prevention programmes to reduce revictimization incidences.

<u>*Low- and middle-income countries*</u>

In the LMIC context, the main focus of domestic violence interventions is the primary prevention of various forms of domestic violence. Findings show that it is possible to reduce the prevalence of violence, with some interventions reaching substantial positive effects within the timeframe of the programmes. There is good evidence that well-designed, long-term, and more intensive interventions, primarily when also addressing alcohol abuse, effectively reduce women's experiences of IPV. Examples are the

Indashyikirwa programme in Rwanda (Dunkle et al., 2019) and the VATU programme in Zambia (Murray et al., 2019). Recent good examples of effective community mobilisation projects: Transforming Masculinities in DRC (Le Roux et al., 2019), Rural Response System in Ghana (Ogum-Alangea et al., 2019). To effectively reduce IPV, these interventions need a strong design and implementation and multi-year intensive community mobilisation (Kerr-Wilson, 2020).

In the case of child abuse, particularly concerning various harmful traditional practices, impact evaluation reviews show that the community mobilisation programmes offer a potentially effective approach. For example, the TOSTAN programme conducted in Senegal significantly reduced the prevalence of female genital mutilation/cutting practices in participating rural villages. A significant aspect of the programme is that villagers themselves identify priority issues for community action, among which female genital mutilation/cutting and IPV were singled out as critical problems.

Most of the interventions have limited or no impact

Despite the several effective domestic violence programmes, many interventions are ineffective in reaching their primary goals, with little usable accompanying evidence that could be used to determine factors and barriers that were impairing its effects. For example, of all domestic violence interventions examined in one of the most rigorous systematic reviews in the field (Arango et al., 2014), more than two-thirds (67%) had no recorded impact on the targeted domestic violence outcomes. Conversely, around 12% of reviewed studies had an evident significant positive effect. An additional 15% of studies had a positive but 'mixed' effect, indicating that obtained findings were positive on some, but not all, measured outcomes. Finally, in around 4% of assessed interventions, the impact was assessed as significantly negative or identified significant adverse outcomes.

Unintended consequences are a rare but persistent threat

Some programmes evidently lead to unintended consequences for their participants or broader target populations. Although the proportion is relatively small, it is still a reason for concern and additional caution and risk assessment in designing and implementing future domestic violence programmes. For example, it is shown that microfinance/economic empowerment programmes alone do not suffice to decrease IPV-related rates and may increase controlling behaviours. Such findings also illustrate the importance of integrating and conducting a careful impact assessment study of any domestic violence intervention to examine its effectiveness and avoid harming or repeating the same mistakes.

Overall, most of the answers are still unanswered – evidence gaps are abundant

Despite the growing evidence base, the fact that few domestic violence interventions are implementing rigorous impact assessment studies and that even fewer among these are effective means that the field is still primarily characterised by the abundance of evidence gaps. These include:

- *There is much less robust empirical research on the effectiveness of domestic violence interventions coming from LMIC contexts.*
- *There is a considerable difference in the number of studies across different research areas.*
- *Some areas, such as micro-finance interventions, receive much more attention than complex and multi-component programmes to transform system-level discrimination or change social norms.*
- *Limited evidence exists on the effectiveness of intervention programmes with particularly vulnerable groups of women and girls, such as the elderly, LGBT populations, people living with disabilities, chronic illness, people belonging to various ethnic or religious minorities, etc.*
- *There is little empirical evidence on domestic violence intervention effectiveness in deprived or conflict regions.*

- *Very few evaluations assessed the impact of domestic violence beyond their respondent groups, at the broader community or population levels.*
- *We know very little or, in many cases, nothing regarding the medium- to the long-term effectiveness of various domestic violence programmes.*
- *Few interventions examine the mechanism of change or the influence of related risk factors, resulting in little usable knowledge on this crucial question.*
- *Very few studies examined the cost-effectiveness or the optimal intensity of their interventions concerning the desired outcomes.*

Relatively poor quality of available empirical evidence

Apart from the limited quantity, there are many severe methodological flaws in the accumulated empirical evidence. The quality of evidence collected in reviewed studies is impaired due to their limited methodological consistency, rigour, quality of employed evaluation standards and processes, assessment methods and research methodologies. Conducted impact assessment studies were often based on a poor general understanding of the impact mechanism, targeted outcomes and various moderating and risk factors in the intervention process. Furthermore, impact assessments were often conducted with small sample sizes and inappropriate and unreliable outcome measures, with no effective control of potential confounding factors. Furthermore, almost all evaluated programmes measured only short-term outcomes, thus failing to provide information on the medium to long-term outcomes, even though these were usually their primary programme objectives. As a result of these quality issues, even the observed positive effects of some of the domestic violence policy interventions have to be interpreted carefully, requiring repeated empirical confirmation across different contexts and over a more extended period. These limitations also point out the need for significant improvements in the impact assessment approaches in the domestic violence programmes, which will require more internal team resources and programme funding for this crucial aspect of programme implementations.

There is insufficient evidence for scaling up good practices

The limited amount of empirical evidence, various quality issues limiting its validity and the limited number of studies with identified positive outcomes restrict accumulation and scaling up the evidence base. The fact that few impact assessment studies examine their effects across broader population groups or different contexts further prevents their findings' generalisability. Moreover, the entire field is still characterised by little understanding of the processes and mechanisms of interventions to achieve their desired changes. Also, as a relatively recent field of research, there is an excellent variety of intervention approaches and impact assessment designs, with considerable heterogeneity of used outcomes and their measures. These factors further prevent comparability of the results across domestic violence programmes and extrapolation of some empirical insights that could inform new interventions. Such a situation also leads to many "conflicting" results, where effects across the similar interventions on the same outcome are opposing or inconsistent and where effects on various outcomes within the same study are both positive and negative.

Future directions

In general, the review of the state of available empirical evidence in this area shows that it is still in its infancy and needs more investment into building a better research infrastructure. Collection of more robust empirical evidence is especially needed in those areas where the gaps are currently the biggest, e.g., in the conflict areas, in cases of intersectoral vulnerabilities, in LMIC contexts. Furthermore, impact evaluation of domestic violence programmes has to start implementing a stricter design to avoid various quality issues and offer clear and valid evaluations of their impact. Domestic violence programmes should also be able to provide evidence on the potential scope and limitations of their scalability regarding both potential target populations and social contexts. Related to the issue of their scalability is also the issue of their cost-effectiveness, which deserves much more attention in future domestic violence programmes and their impact assessments. Such considerations would greatly contribute to the better allocation of available resources and general improvement in the accountability and effectiveness of domestic violence programmes.

Abbreviations and acronyms

BIP Batterer intervention programmes

CAM Child abuse and maltreatment

CSA Child sexual abuse

CBO Community-based organisation

CBT Cognitive behavioural therapy

CM Child marriage

CPV Child peer violence

CSA Child Sexual Abuse

DFID Department for International Development

FGM Female genital mutilation

FSW Female Sex Workers

GBV Gender-based violence

HIC High Income Countries

HTP Harmful traditional practices

ICT Information and communications technology

IPV Intimate partner violence

LMIC Low- and middle-income countries

NPSA Non-partner sexual assault

PSM Propensity score matching

RCT Randomised controlled trial

RDD Regression discontinuity design

SR Systematic review

VAWG Violence against women and girls

UN United Nations

WHO World Health Organization

1. Introduction

Domestic violence (DV) was long overlooked, ignored or underestimated. It was not until the last decade of the 20th century that most countries worldwide started focusing on this issue and introducing lawful protections against it in their legal systems. In the last decade, increased attention has been placed on various forms of domestic violence, including its most prevalent form of intimate partner violence (IPV), child abuse and other more specific forms of violence such as honour killings or forced marriages.

Increased attention to the issue was followed by a growing number of intervention programmes to prevent the occurrence or reoccurrence of various forms of domestic violence. Unfortunately, in the beginning, these interventions often did not employ rigorous evaluation designs that would assess their effectiveness. Instead, they mainly relied on anecdotal accounts and untested assumptions. However, this is slowly changing in the last decade, with an increasing number of programmes using systematic empirical methods to evaluate their impact on target outcomes.

As discussed in Volume 1 of this series (*Policy and Research on Gender Equality: An Overview[1]*), there is an important data gap in the last stage of the 'data value chain' – in the measurement of the impact of various policy interventions. This is because there are fewest stakeholders engaged in this stage. The least amount of resources is available, and it generally receives less attention than any other data collection stage. Yet, without robust data on the effectiveness of domestic violence interventions, we will not be able to introduce positive change in this area and thus reduce the incidence of domestic violence. This is why, in this report, we will try to present and evaluate existing empirical evidence

---

1. *https://books2read.com/u/mBzEYy*

on the effectiveness of interventions in the field of domestic violence gathered around the world so far. In other words, we will try to answer "what works," i.e. what is known to be an effective intervention strategy, under which conditions, and for which outcomes.

The report is based on an extensive literature review and summarises the findings presented in various systematic reviews and meta-analyses published over the last few years. The report aims to offer a comprehensive overview of the evidence, including relevant findings from the entire selected literature. As such, it is more extensive than any of the reviewed papers and reports. We prioritised compiling evidence from rigorous empirical studies using experimental (i.e. randomised controlled trials – RCTs) and quasi-experimental designs. However, we also included a few studies with other designs, reviewed in some selected meta-analyses.

In the remainder of this chapter, we will shortly discuss various forms of domestic and family violence, their prevalence, and their consequences. In chapter two, we will outline some of the critical characteristics of domestic violence interventions. Main empirical findings on the effectiveness of domestic violence interventions will be presented in chapter three, followed by the evaluation of limitations and gaps in presented evidence in chapter four.

Forms and prevalence of domestic violence

"Domestic violence" (also called "domestic abuse") is violence or other abuse that occurs in a domestic setting, such as a marriage or cohabitation. Domestic violence is often synonymous with "family violence" or "intimate partner violence". However, in this report, we will distinguish between these terms, which, although greatly overlapping, still indicate somewhat distinct forms of violence. In particular, IPV refers to any behaviour in an intimate relationship that causes physical, sexual, or psychological harm, including aggression, sexual coercion, psychological abuse and controlling behaviour (WHO, 2005). IPV usually occurs in domestic settings, therefore being a form of domestic violence. Still, it can also happen outside of domestic environments, e.g. during dating relationships or in non-cohabitating relationships, in which cases it doesn't belong to domestic violence. Likewise, family violence is abuse or violence between family members or relatives. Although often committed within the domestic setting, thus broadly corresponding with domestic violence, family violence can also happen outside of this setting, e.g. between family members who belong to different households. In the remainder of this report, we will refer to domestic violence as an umbrella term for all forms of domestic, family and intimate partner violence while still acknowledging the subtle differences between these terms.

Domestic violence is a widespread form of abuse worldwide (**Figure 1**). It is assumed that domestic violence is one of the most underreported crimes against both women and men. Globally, the victims of domestic violence are overwhelmingly women, and women tend to experience more severe forms of violence. They are also likelier than men to use intimate partner violence in self-defence. There is a strong relationship between the level of gender equality and the incidence of domestic violence in a given country with less domestic violence occurring in countries with a higher level of gender equality (Esquivel-Santoveña et al., 2013).

Figure 1: Global prevalence estimates of violence against women and girls

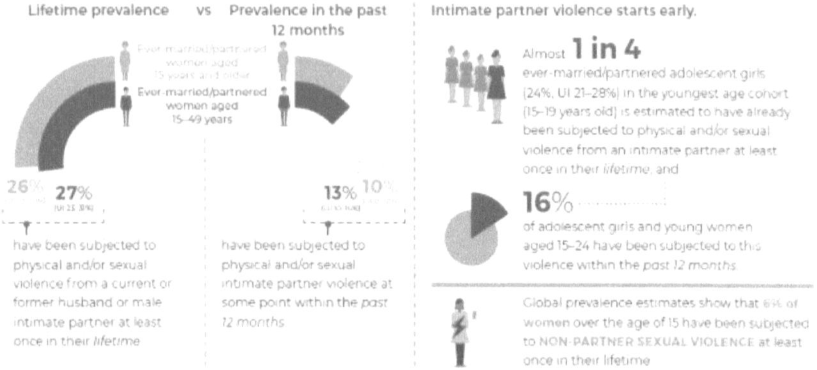

Source: WHO (2018). Global Fact Sheet. Violence Against Women: Prevalence Estimates[2], 2018.

Domestic violence occurs between household members and takes many forms, including sexual, physical, and psychological abuse. Intimate partner violence (IPV) is one of the most common forms of VAWG. It refers to acts and behaviour of the current or previous husband, boyfriend, or another partner that causes physical, sexual or psychological harm. It includes physical aggression, sexual coercion, psychological abuse and controlling behaviours. Such violence both reflects and reinforces underlying gender-based inequalities.

Domestic or family violence also includes various forms of child abuse by a parent, guardian or siblings. In addition, child abuse may consist of any act or failure to act by a parent or a caregiver that results in actual or potential harm to a child. Although child abuse can happen outside of their homes (e.g. perpetrated by strangers), in this report, we will focus on those instances in which child abuse occurs within domestic settings.

Elder abuse is another form of domestic violence defined as "a single, or repeated act, or lack of appropriate action, occurring within any relationship where there is an expectation of trust, which causes harm or distress to an older person." (WHO, 2002). Elder violence can commit

2. https://apps.who.int/iris/rest/bitstreams/1349966/retrieve

people who are known and have a relationship with a victim or people they rely upon for their care or services. Almost all forms of elder abuse and violence occur in domestic settings, thus falling under domestic violence. However, elder abuse is not always a form of family violence, as paid caregivers and other non-relatives can also be perpetrators of this form of violence. Nursing home abuse is a particular form of elder violence occurring when abused elder persons live in nursing home settings.

Harmful traditional practices represent another form of domestic violence when they occur in domestic settings. These practices differ across cultures and include female genital mutilation, acid throwing, honour killing, dowry killing, bride burning, etc.

Other forms of abuse and violence occurring in domestic and family settings include violence committed against people with disabilities, violence against LGBTI+ people, violence between siblings, violence between roommates/housemates, etc. Definitions of the primary forms of domestic and family violence discussed in this report are outlined in **Table 1**.

Table 1: Description of the primary forms of domestic violence

Domestic violence

Domestic violence (also called domestic abuse) is violence or other abuse that occurs in a domestic setting, such as in a marriage or cohabitation. The main form of domestic violence is intimate partner violence, but it also implicates violence against children, parents, the elderly, or other household members. DV includes physical, verbal, emotional, economic, religious, reproductive, or sexual abuse. The latter ranges from subtle, coercive forms to marital rape and physical violence (e.g. choking, beating, female genital mutilation, and acid throwing) that may result in disfigurement or death.

Family violence

Family violence is any threatening, coercive, dominating or abusive behaviour between people in a family, domestic or (current or former) intimate relationship that causes a person to experience fear. Family violence is often thought to occur between intimate partners or immediate relations living in the same home. But family violence can also be perpetrated by someone who lives with the victim in a "family-like relationship" (e.g. a carer) or in relationships culturally recognised by the community as "family-like" (such as Aboriginal communities).

Intimate partner violence

IPV refers to any behaviour in an intimate relationship that causes physical, sexual, or psychological harm, including aggression, sexual coercion, psychological abuse and controlling behaviour (WHO, 2005). An intimate partner is a person with whom an individual has a close, personal relationship characterised by emotional connectedness, regular contact or sexual behaviour, identification as a couple, and cohabitation. Intimate partners may include current or former

	spouses, boyfriends or girlfriends, dating partners, and ongoing sexual partners (Breiding et al., 2015).
Child abuse or maltreatment	Child abuse or maltreatment constitutes all forms of physical and emotional ill-treatment, sexual abuse, neglect, negligent treatment, and commercial or other exploitation. Such abuse can result in actual or potential harm to the child's health, survival, development, or dignity in the context of a relationship of responsibility, trust or power (WHO, 1999).
Elder abuse	Elder abuse is "a single, or repeated act, or lack of appropriate action, occurring within any relationship where there is an expectation of trust, which causes harm or distress to an older person." Elder abuse is a form of domestic or nursing home violence and can be perpetrated by family members/cohabitants or caregivers.
Harmful traditional practices (within domestic settings)	Any incident of violence perpetrated in the name of social, cultural or religious values. It includes female genital mutilation, acid throwing, honour killing, dowry killing, bride burning, etc.
Parental violence	Parental violence is abusive or violent behaviour towards a parent by their children or dependent persons.
Dating abuse	Dating violence is abusive or violent behaviour used by a casual partner against the other partner.
Violence against people with disabilities	Violence against people with disabilities is a form of domestic violence when the perpetrator is a member of the victim's family or household. People with disabilities experience violence at higher rates than people without disabilities. In particular, women with a disability are at

> greater risk. Women with a disability may also
> experience barriers to accessing support services.

Consequences of domestic violence

Like all forms of violence or abuse, domestic violence has many detrimental consequences on its victims and entire families and households. Domestic violence is especially harmful because it is perpetrated in the most intimate settings by close family members. Furthermore, victims of domestic violence are often exposed to various forms of abuse throughout an extended period, which make for more damaging and long-term effects. Finally, victims of domestic abuse are often economically, socially or emotionally dependent on their abusers, which makes them more vulnerable and significantly prolongs the period and severity of abuse before they find a way to escape or report the abuse.

Consequently, domestic violence often leaves long-term consequences on victims' physical, mental, and emotional health and well-being. In addition, domestic violence also incurs high psychological, social and economic costs on affected families and societies as a whole. In most severe cases, domestic violence can have fatal outcomes, such as the homicide of a perpetrator or a victim or victim's suicide. IPV leads to direct injuries in 42% of affected women (WHO, 2013). Sexual violence and abuse can lead to unintended pregnancies, induced abortions, reproductive problems, and the transmission of STDs, including HIV. For example, sexually abused women are twice as likely to have an abortion (WHO, 2013). Furthermore, women who experience IPV are 16% more likely to suffer a miscarriage and 41% more likely to have a premature birth (WHO, 2013).

Victims of domestic violence are also more likely to experience depression, post-traumatic stress disorder, sleep difficulties, eating disorders, and attempt suicide (WHO, 2013). Sexual violence, especially the one experienced during childhood or adolescence, can lead to substance abuse, drinking problems, and risky sexual behaviours. It is also associated with a higher likelihood of being a victim of violence later in life. New research illustrates strong associations between exposure to DV and abuse in all their forms and higher rates of many chronic conditions (Breiding et al., 2015). The Adverse Childhood Experiences Study has shown a relationship between exposure to abuse or neglect and higher rates in adulthood of chronic conditions, high-risk health behaviours and shortened life span (Middlebrooks et al., 2008).

As mentioned, domestic violence also damages victims' families. Children who grow up in families with intimate-partner violence can show various behavioural and emotional difficulties associated with their experience of witnessing domestic violence. These experiences can also have long-term consequences on their physical and mental health and their likelihood of perpetrating or experiencing violence later in life. The broader social and economic costs of domestic violence are enormous and have indirect effects throughout society. For example, victims of domestic violence can be isolated and withdrawn from closer social circles; they are less likely to participate in regular activities and have reduced capacity to care for themselves and their children. Victims of domestic violence are also less likely to work and, in general, to take advantage of economic opportunities (International Rescue Committee [IRC], 2012).

2. Interventions preventing domestic violence

Prevalence of domestic violence interventions

Programmes aiming to prevent domestic violence have started to occur in the last decade of the 20th century and have significantly accelerated during the previous decade. At the same time, an increasing number of these interventions have applied elaborate impact assessments, thus slowly building up the evidence base of their effectiveness. This growing evidence base is well illustrated in the systematic review of IPV interventions by Picon and colleagues (2017) (**Figure 2**). The figure also shows that most of the reviewed empirical evidence comes from recent studies.

Figure 2: Number of VAWG interventions in law to middle-income countries between 2006 - 2016

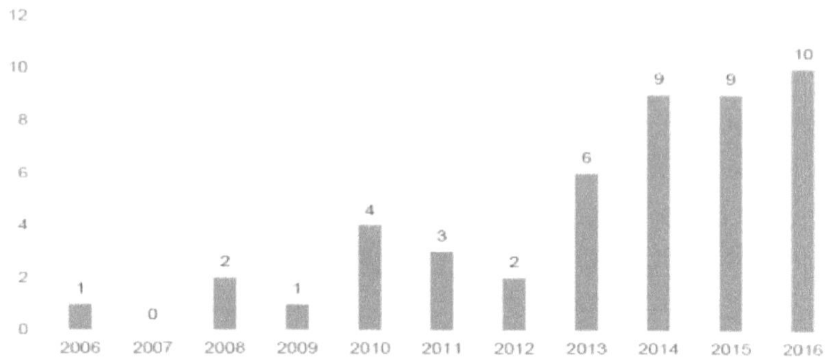

Source: Picon et al. (2017). Intimate partner violence prevention: an evidence gap map, 3ie Evidence Gap Map Report 8. International Initiative for Impact Evaluation (3ie).

Forms of Violence Studied

Most of the programmes in the area of domestic violence focus on intimate partner violence as the most prevalent form of domestic violence. An illustration of the dominance of IPV interventions among other forms of domestic violence and violence against women and girls is presented in **Figure 3**. It shows the distribution of reviews according to the form of violence addressed in the World Bank's systematic review of VAWG (Arango et al., 2014). A majority of the reviews (59%) examined interventions aimed at reducing IPV. Around a quarter of the studies analysed evidence related to the reduction of non-partner sexual abuse. The additional 9% (five reviews) focused on findings related to several types of violence women and girls face. Two reviews related to harmful traditional practices (HTP), and only one of the selected 58 reviews solely examined female genital mutilation/cutting (FGM/C), child marriage (CM), trafficking and child sexual abuse.

Figure 3: Type of violence reviewed

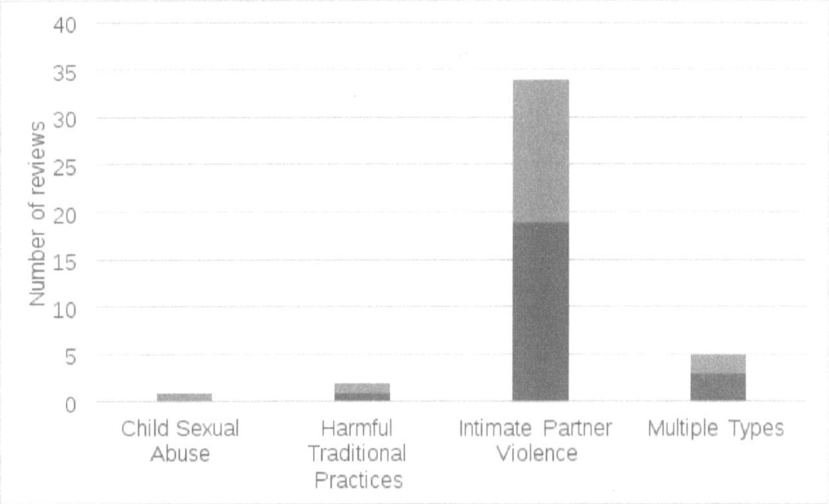

Source: Arango, Diana & Morton, Matthew & Gennari, Floriza & Kiplesund, Sveinung & Ellsberg, Mary (2014). Interventions to prevent or reduce violence against women and girls: A systematic review of reviews. http://dx.doi.org/10.13140/RG.2.1.2545.6168

Geographic distribution of the domestic violence interventions

The majority of the reviewed domestic violence interventions identified in the literature were conducted in the high-income countries in North America, Western Europe, and the Pacific region (Arango et al., 2014; Ellsberg et al., 2014). Moreover, even within the high-income context, the distribution is skewed, with two-thirds of all selected studies coming from the United States.

However, although most of the selected studies were conducted in high-income countries, this pattern is not consistent across individual categories of domestic violence (**Figure 4**). For example, most studies focused on harmful traditional practices are implemented in the LMIC context, reflecting the fact that such practices are more common in these countries. Likewise, most primary prevention programmes are implemented in LMICs, while VAWG interventions in high-income countries often focus on secondary prevention (Ellsberg et al., 2014).

Figure 4: Number of selected studies by countries' income level

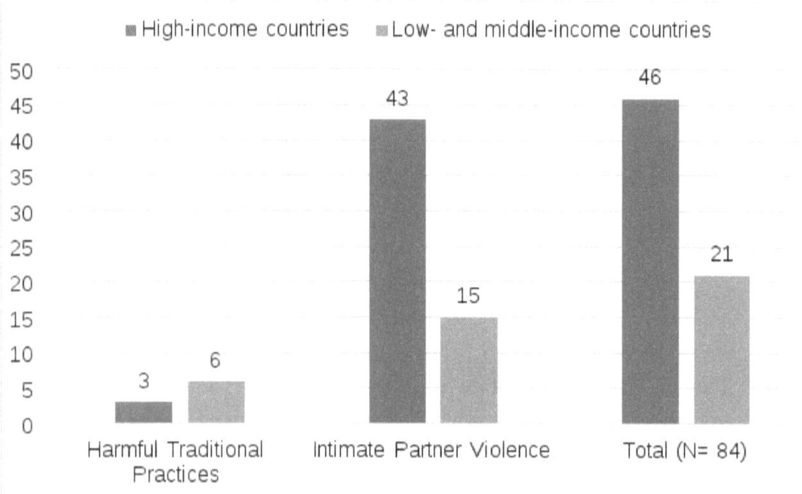

Source: Adjusted from Arango, Diana & Morton, Matthew & Gennari, Floriza & Kiplesund, Sveinung & Ellsberg, Mary (2014). Interventions to prevent or reduce violence against women and girls: A systematic review of reviews. http://dx.doi.org/10.13140/RG.2.1.2545.6168

Types of domestic violence interventions

Many intervention strategies have been used in domestic violence interventions, focusing on primary prevention (before violence occurs) or secondary intervention (after violence occurs). The interventions focus on individual, group, community or system-wide levels. Among these are 1) one-on-one individual therapy or training sessions, 2) work with couples and families, 3) group-based interventions (e.g. group training), 4) community mobilisation efforts, 5) "gender transformative" programmes that aim to change system-wide social norms, gender roles and stereotypes, embedded power structures and institutional and economic inequalities. Most domestic violence interventions focus on primary or secondary prevention of IPV. But an increasing number of them are expanding their focus to other forms of domestic violence. In particular, there is a small but growing number of programmes on domestic child abuse, elderly abuse, parental abuse, residential care abuse, abuse of persons with disabilities, abuse of pregnant women, abuse of LGBTI+ persons, etc.

Domestic violence interventions can be categorised across several criteria. First, many systematic reviews classify DV interventions based on the victim's profile, thus distinguishing between domestic abuse of women (IPV), children, elderly, parents, etc. Second, DV interventions are often classified across the geographical and socio-economic contexts in which they are implemented, with reviews focusing on interventions in LMICs (e.g., Picon et al., 2017 and Pundir et al., 2020) or in specific regions, such as South America or Sub-Saharan countries (e.g., Bott et al., 2019).

Third, interventions are also differentiated according to the types of domestic violence or their approaches, thus distinguishing between many forms of violence and DV programmes outlined in **Appendix 1**. A critical distinction between DV interventions is whether they focus on the victim or the perpetrator of the violence. The majority of the interventions in the Global North have been directed towards women and children as potential or actual victims of domestic violence. However, an increasing number of interventions are turning attention to DV perpetrators (Kelly & Westmarland, 2015). Research shows that many of them tend to repeat their violence (Hester and Westmarland, 2005).

Furthermore, the usual route of persecuting the perpetrators through the criminal justice system has made little difference in changing their behaviours (CPS, 2014). Finally, an important distinction between the types of DV interventions is based on whether the programme is implemented before or after such violence occurs. Primary intervention programmes aim to reduce the likelihood of DV occurring, while secondary intervention programmes have the dual goal of providing support to the victims of violence and helping prevent its reoccurrence.

Prevalence of different types of DV interventions

In **Figure 5**, we present the distribution of reviewed DV interventions in one of the systematic reviews of their effectiveness and the information on the primary or secondary types of preventions. Some interventions are characteristic of specific forms of domestic violence. For example, batterer interventions (reducing recidivism among perpetrators of violence) are the most common in the IPV category. On the other hand, livelihood interventions and community mobilisation in primary prevention were the most frequent intervention methods in the harmful traditional practices category. The prevalence of DV interventions across several other characteristics is presented in **Appendix 2**.

Figure 5: Number of selected studies by type of intervention

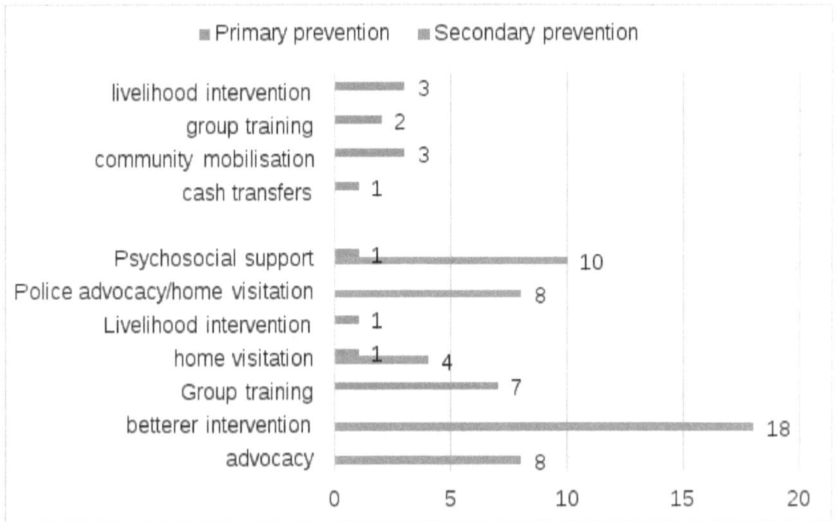

Source: Adjusted from Arango et al. (2014). Interventions to prevent or reduce violence against women and girls: A systematic review of reviews. http://dx.doi.org/10.13140/RG.2.1.2545.6168

Systematic reviews of Intervention programs

With the growth of the DV interventions, there is an increasing need for systematic reviews of their effectiveness and impact. Over the recent years, several systematic overviews of the empirical evidence in this area have been published. However, none of them is exclusively and comprehensively focused on all forms of domestic violence. Furthermore, most of the available reviews focus on specific domains of evidence, either in terms of geographic regions, particular intervention strategies or particular forms of domestic violence. In general, we can divide the available literature on the effectiveness of DV intervention programmes into three groups.

Within <u>the first group</u> of the comprehensive reviews tackling all forms of violence against women and girls, the most rigorous and systematic are the two reviews published in 2014. The first is a policy report commissioned by the World Bank (WB) and conducted by Arango and colleagues (2014). The second is an academic article written by Ellsberg and colleagues (2014) and published in the leading scientific journal Lancet. These are the first systematic reviews of reviews that synthesise evidence on the effects of VAWG prevention interventions. Notably, most of the selected reviewed evidence concerns various forms of domestic violence, including IPV, child abuse and harmful traditional practices. Another two comprehensive reviews were published at the beginning and the end of the DFID's programme *"What Works to Prevent Violence Against Women and Girls"*. The first one is Fulu and colleagues (2015) review, which was composed as a baseline overview of the available evidence at the programme's start. However, the authors did not implement a systematic review and did not use standard criteria to evaluate programme effectiveness. The second "What Works" review was prepared by Kerr-Wilson and colleagues (2020). It complements the review of Fulu and colleagues (2015) with new research studies and empirical evidence and implements a more thorough and systematic approach. However, it was still not as rigorous and scientifically sound as the World Bank review since it did not implement some of the established scientific criteria for evaluating the effectiveness of reviewed interventions. Instead, the authors relied on their ad hoc evaluation criteria. However, both DFID reports are highly informative and offer a wealth of new information that directly complements the World Bank reports from 2014.

The second group of sources consists of systematic reviews focused exclusively on particular forms of domestic violence. Picon and colleagues (2017) from *The International Initiative for Impact Evaluation (3ie)* published a systematic review of available empirical evidence on IPV interventions. Although bringing further insight into the characteristics and prevalence of IPV interventions in LMIC contexts, this review brought relatively limited information on the effectiveness of these interventions and the factors affecting their outcomes. Pundir and colleagues (2020) recently published a systematic review of the interventions for reducing violence against children. This review focused on the programmes conducted in LMICs, most of which were from Sub-Saharan Africa. Although limited in scope, the review is significant in offering the first systematic summary of findings in child abuse interventions in disadvantaged contexts.

Finally, the third group of reviews consisted of meta-analyses focused on particular DV intervention approaches or target populations. Examples of such reviews are Karakurt and colleagues' (2019) meta-analysis of the effectiveness of the interventions on perpetrators of IPV or Rivas and colleagues (2019), and Cohran's review of the impact of advocacy interventions against various forms of VAWG. Furthermore, Jahanfar and colleagues' (2014) systematic review of interventions preventing DV against pregnant women or Ribeiro and colleagues' (2021) integrative review of the interventions preventing violence against the older adults also belong to this group.

Most of the presented systematic reviews tried to select only those impact assessment studies that have used more rigorous evaluation designs in the forms of either experiments or quasi-experiments. The main characteristics of the six systematic reviews serving as a basis of our report are outlined in **Table 2.**

Table 2: Characteristics of the systematic evidence reviews in the area of domestic violence

	Arango et al (2014)	Ellsberg et al (2014)	Fulu et al (2015)	Kerr-Wilson et al (2020)	Picon et al (2017)	Picon et al (2017)
Type of review	Systematic review or reviews	Systematic review or reviews	Rapid review (non-systematic)	Systematic review or reviews	Systematic review or reviews	Systematic review or reviews
Scope	Global	Global	Global	Global with emphasis on LMICs	LMICs	LMICs
Type of violence	VAWG	VAWG	VAWG: IPV, NPA, CSA, CAM	VAWG: IPV, NPA, CPV	Primary IPV interventions	Corporal punishment, IPV, peer violence
Criteria for inclusion	RCT; quasi-experiments	RCT; quasi-experiments	Any type of impact evaluation	RCT; quasi-exp.; 'What Works' studies	RCT; quasi-exp; PSM; RDD; SR	RCT; quasi-exp; PSM; RDD; SR
Number of reviews	58	58	24	12	0	55
Number of individual interventions	84	84	244	104	47 (+28 ongoing)	152
Quality evaluation criteria	Strict	Strict	Loose	Loose	Moderate	Strict
Time period of evaluation	200 - 2013	200 - 2013	200 - 2014	2000 - 2019	2000 - 2016	2000 - 2019
Funded by	World Bank	World Bank & Australian government	DFID (What Works to Prevent Violence)	DFID (What Works to Prevent Violence)	The International Initiative for Impact Evaluation (3ie)	UNICEF
Published as	Policy report	Academic paper	Policy report	Policy report	Policy report	Policy report

Note: SR-Systematic Reviews; PSM - Propensity Score Matching: RDD - Regression Discontinuity Design; IPV - Intimate partner violence; NPA - non-partner abuse; CSA - child sexual abuse; CAM - child abuse & maltreatment; CPV - child peer violence.

3. Main findings from reviews – sorted by the category of violence

Of all the 84 interventions using an experimental or quasi-experimental study design and summarised in included World Bank reviews, the overwhelming majority (70%) had no recorded impact on the targeted VAWG outcomes (Arango et al., 2014; Ellsberg et al., 2014). Around one in ten reviewed studies had an evident significant positive effect. An additional 14% of studies had a positive but "mixed" effect, indicating that obtained findings were positive on some, but not all, measured outcomes. Finally, in around 5% of assessed interventions, the impact was assessed as significantly negative or identified significant adverse outcomes (**Figure 6**).

Figure 6: Impact assessment across selected studies by type of violence

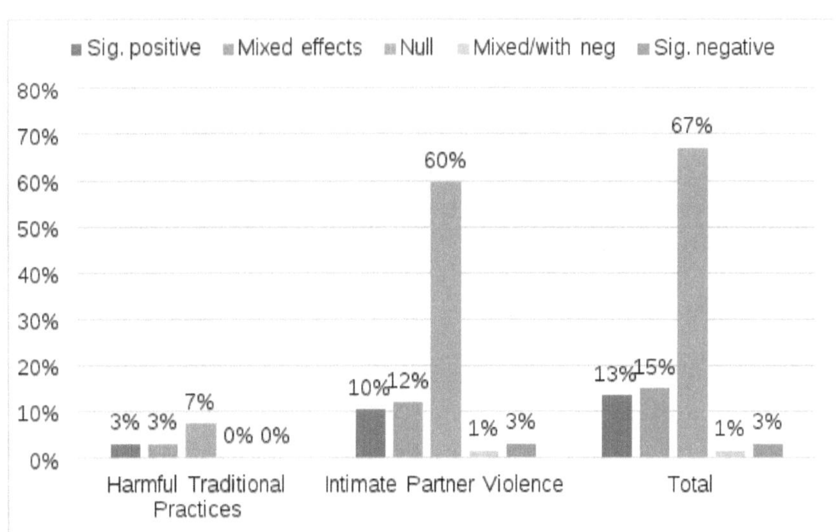

Source: Adjusted from Arango et al. (2014). Interventions to prevent or reduce violence against women and girls: A systematic review of reviews. http://dx.doi.org/10.13140/RG.2.1.2545.6168

The two meta-analytic studies of the effectiveness of VAWG interventions (Arango et al., 2014; Ellsberg et al., 2014) provide a valuable overview of the findings of VAWG program effectiveness across different categories of violence and country income levels. Additionally, two What Works' global evidence reviews (Fulu et al., 2015; Kerr-Wilson et al., 2020) cover more recent effectiveness studies and portray some of the successful VAWG intervention programmes in more detail. Key findings from these overviews will be presented in the following paragraphs.

3.1 Intimate Partner Violence

A large number of impact evaluations (19 comprehensive and 15 systematic reviews) address IPV. The majority of interventions in this field took place in **high-income countries** and focused on **secondary prevention approaches** (i.e. prevention of reoccurrence), namely:

- batterer interventions (centred on men/perpetrators; generally lack positive effects on VAWG),
- survivor services (centred on women/survivors; mixed results; in particular, intensive advocacy services and psychosocial support have positive results).

Evaluated interventions generally scored as of moderate quality: sample sizes tended to be small; sampling strategies were unclear; there is a lack of data on the cost-effectiveness of interventions, and the impact of working in a multisectoral manner was not sufficiently measured.

In terms of intervention classification, we combined the approaches provided in Arango et al. (2014) and Fulu et al. (2015) to understand better which type of intervention prevails in which economic context. So, besides primary and secondary interventions, we distinguish between the following categories:

1. **Individual-level interventions** primarily target individuals or individual-level change. Even though some of these interventions are implemented through groups, they focus on changing individual risk factors for violence, such as alcohol abuse and economic or social disempowerment.

2. **Group-based interventions** include empowerment programmes for women and girls, training tackling gender norms with men and boys, alternative rites of passage, and family-level interventions addressing couples' relationship dynamics and promoting positive parenting practices.

3. **Population-level interventions** include community mobilisation, awareness-raising campaigns, social marketing campaigns or edutainment, and economic empowerment and livelihood programmes.

4. **System-wide interventions** include broadly (usually nationally) implemented IPV screening in hospitals, home visitation programmes, justice and law-enforcement interventions, training for health workers and other personnel, etc.

3.1.1 Primary Prevention Interventions

Primary prevention aims to reduce the number of new instances of violence by intervening before violence takes place. In addition, these interventions aspire to foster societies, communities, organisations, and relationships in which violence is less likely to occur (e.g., through challenging attitudes and practices that justify, excuse, or condone violence).

Primary prevention approaches have been studied less frequently than secondary prevention. Nevertheless, encouraging results emerge from this type of intervention applied in the middle- and low-income settings.

3.1.1.1 High-income countries (HICs)

Approaches to address IPV as characteristic in HICs contexts include:

1. on the **individual level**: perinatal and antenatal care, family planning, parenting programmes, advocacy, reduction of alcohol abuse, and
2. on the **group level**: school-based interventions addressing dating violence and bystander behaviours.

Four evaluations with positive findings include a Hawaiian perinatal home visiting program, a reproductive coercion evaluation in California, and two group training programmes on "Healthy Relationships" in Canada, conducted with male and female high school students or at-risk youth (Arango et al., 2014). More recent "What works" reports also cover school-based interventions conducted in US schools, working with men and boys only at US universities and tackling alcohol abuse in Australia (Fulu et al., 2015; Kerr-Wilson et al.,2020).

Home visitations (HV): traditionally used to monitor pregnancy, protect the health of pregnant women and infants, and improve parenting skills. Conducted almost exclusively in HICs, these interventions include: 1) psycho-behavioural counselling, safety planning, legal and financial advice, and 2) nurse-visitation programmes during and after pregnancy. Given their close contact with women, HV programmes could potentially reduce IPV, but limited evidence of their effectiveness is available so far. However, further research is urged in this field to make the role of home-visiting nurses more effective in IPV prevention.

> <u>Main findings</u>: During the implementation of Hawaii's Healthy Start Program (HSP) (Duggan et al., 1999), mothers in the intervention group reported significantly lower IPV

victimisation rates than mothers in the control group (Arango et al., 2014).

Advocacy: Reproductive coercion includes pregnancy coercion (e.g. male partners' verbal pressure to get women pregnant) and active interference with contraceptive methods (birth control sabotage). It increases the risk of unintended pregnancy, HIV and other sexually transmitted infections.

<u>Main findings</u>: An intervention conducted in four family-planning clinics in Northern California found a 71 per cent decrease in the odds of pregnancy coercion among women in the intervention group compared to participants in the control clinics. Women in the intervention arm were also more likely to report ending unhealthy relationships (Arango et al., 2014).

School-based interventions: There is good evidence that school-based interventions can prevent dating violence. The more effective interventions involved extended programmes delivered by highly trained facilitators or teachers, used participatory learning approaches (including critical reflection and skills building) and were based on theories of gender and power. They were also evaluated with long-term follow-up. More research is needed to develop interventions to use more effectively in classrooms, especially in LMIC settings, and ensure the impact on girls and boys. (Kerr-Wilson, 2020).

<u>Main findings</u>: The two mentioned Canadian programmes on "Healthy Relationships" (Wolfe et al., 2009) showed significant reductions in dating violence perpetration in the intervention group compared to the control groups (Arango et al., 2014). The "Green dot" bystander training in US high schools (Coker et al., 2017) is a more recent example of

school-based interventions in the HICs with positive findings on dating violence (Kerr-Wilson, 2020).

Working with men and boys only: 1) participatory educational programmes that promote positive masculinity and 2) bystander interventions in schools and sports teams mainly applied in US universities (Kerr-Wilson, 2020).

Main findings: Out of 13 assessed interventions (in Fulu et al., 2015), only one found positive outcomes (Coaching Boys into Men, Miller et al., 2012) in terms of reduced bystander support of negative behaviour of peers and, consequently, less abuse perpetration.

Tackling alcohol abuse: Interventions applied on various levels, including 1) screening in primary care settings, and early detection; 2) restricted access to alcohol (laws, policies, prices); 3) community-based interventions and public dialogue, changing the drinking environment; 4) treatment and self-help support systems, such as AA; CBT-based couples' interventions.

Main findings: There is fair evidence from HICs that structural alcohol reduction interventions positively impact reducing IPV (e.g. a longitudinal study conducted in Australia, Livingston et al., 2008). However, many detoxification treatments and couple therapies that proved successful in HIC are not affordable in LMIC. On the other hand, the low-cost model of self-help groups (e.g. implemented through religious organisations in Latin America) does not allow evaluation through RCT as it contradicts their philosophy of being open to everybody. Nevertheless, propensity score matching showed significant effects of this model of interventions (Fulu et al., 2015).

3.1.1.2 Low- and Middle-Income Countries

In the low- and middle-income countries, costly individual-level primary interventions are rarely conducted on a larger scale. Interventions that prevail in LMICs are:

1. **group-level** training programmes (for men only, women only, or men and women together, including group training for couples) and
2. **population-level** interventions, such as livelihood programmes and direct transfers of food and money.

Most primary violence prevention programmes in LMIC contexts use participatory group training, which involves a series of educational meetings or workshops with targeted groups of participants (Ellsberg, 2014). Multi-component interventions also include social communication (e.g. radio and television spots, billboards, theatre), community mobilisation and livelihood strategies. These programmes are often embedded in broader interventions that aim to improve the health and wellbeing of women and girls. Their goal is usually broader than just preventing violence, often including components to address underlying gender norms and stereotypes and promote the development of new communication and conflict resolution skills.

Empowerment training for women and girls: School or community programmes to improve women's agency. It can include other components such as safe spaces, mentoring, life skills, or self-defence training. These programmes address IPV and other forms of VAWG, such as child marriages and female genital mutilations.

Group training for women and men: School or community workshops to promote changes in norms and behaviour that encourage violence against women and girls and gender inequality. Many of the interventions emerged from HIV reduction programmes, with the growing recognition of gender inequality and IPV as drivers of HIV infection.

> Main findings: Stepping Stones, a program applied in 70 villages in South Africa, uses participatory learning approaches to build knowledge, risk awareness, and communication and relationship skills relating to gender, violence and HIV. Two years following an intervention, men's self-reported perpetration of physical and sexual IPV was significantly lower compared to men in the control villages (p=0.05). Still, no differences were found in women's reports of IPV victimisation (Jewkes et al., 2008).

Group training for men and boys only: participatory educational programmes that promote positive masculinity. Yaari Dosti intervention targeting young married and unmarried men in Mumbai and Gorakhpur, India, aimed to reduce male-perpetrated VAWG by transforming gender-inequitable norms through group training and "social lifestyle marketing" (Verma et al., 2008, cited in Arango et al., 2014). More recent examples include men's discussions groups in Côte d'Ivoire (Hossain et al., 2014); interactive group education and community mobilisation with young men in Ethiopia (Pulerwitz et al., 2015) and India (Verma et al., 2008), showed good results in reducing IVP (Kerr-Wilson et al., 2020).

> Main findings: In general, the evidence of the effectiveness of these programmes is conflicting in LMICs. In the Yaari Dosti programme, men's self-reported perpetration of physical and sexual IPV was significantly lower compared to participants in the comparison group (p<0.005).

Couples' interventions: Workshops aimed to develop communication and conflict resolution skills, as well as psychological therapies for couples addressing learnt behaviour and childhood trauma (Kerr-Wilson, 2020).

Main findings: There is good evidence that well-designed, long-term and more intensive interventions, primarily when also addressing alcohol abuse, are an effective approach in reducing women's experiences of IPV. Examples are the Indashyikirwa programme in Rwanda (Dunkle et al., 2019) and the VATU programme in Zambia (Murray et al., 2019).

Parenting programmes: Interventions aimed to reduce harsh parenting and child abuse, a risk factor for VAW later in life. These interventions include home visits, counselling in health clinic settings based on educational communication, role play, and guided play between parents and children.

Main findings: Although still rare, parenting programmes that explicitly address IPV show good evidence of effectiveness in reducing IPV in both HICs and LMICs. An example in the LMICs context is the Bandebereho programme in Rwanda (Doyle et al., 2018).

School-based (institutional) interventions: The teaching of specific gender-themed curricula, teacher training, gender-responsive pedagogy, children's clubs, as well as engagement of various stakeholders at the school level (teachers, pupils, parents, reporting mechanisms, government).

Main findings: There is insufficient evidence of the effectiveness of these interventions in both HICs and LMICs.

Community mobilisation campaigns: Interventions aiming to reduce violence at the population level through changes in public discourse, practices, and norms for gender and violence (Ellsberg et al., 2014). They involve participatory projects, workshops, peer training and other forms of community-driven development. They have "promising" results in LMIC contexts, while they were either not applicable or had no robust impact evaluations in the high-income countries. Despite their relatively high prevalence (at the global, regional or national level), **awareness-raising campaigns** are found to be ineffective in both low- and high-income contexts. On the other hand, there is insufficient evidence on the efficacy of **social marketing campaigns or edutainment** (education through entertainment activities) across all economic contexts.

> Main findings: Recent good examples of effective community mobilisation projects: Transforming Masculinities in DRC (Le Roux et al., 2019), Rural Response System in Ghana (Ogum-Alangea et al., 2019). To effectively reduce IPV, these interventions need a strong design and implementation and multi-year intensive community mobilisation (Kerr-Wilson, 2020). // Social marketing campaigns (long-term programmes engaging social media, mobile applications, thematic television series, posters, etc.) may have a role when combined with other components of interventions at a community level.

Livelihood programmes: These programmes involve microfinance, vocational training or job placements, and cash or asset transfers (e.g., land reform). Their effectiveness is more promising when including social empowerment components, such as gender equality and violence prevention training. An innovative programme, IMAGE, applied in South Africa, combined microfinance with training and skills-building sessions on preventing HIV infection, gender norms, cultural beliefs, communication, and intimate partner violence (Arango et al.2014). Recent good examples include long-term multi-component programmes for adolescent girls in Uganda (Bandiera et al., 2018) and Kenya (Austrian et al., 2018), which combine microfinance/cash transfers with vocational training and violence prevention discussions. (Kerr-Wilson, 2020).

> Main findings: IMAGE effectiveness evaluation showed a reduction of over 50 per cent in women's reports of physical or sexual violence from a partner in the intervention group compared to the control group. According to Cork et al. (2018), evaluations of microfinance/economic empowerment alone indicate that they do not suffice to decrease IPV-related rates and may increase controlling behaviours (Green et al., 2015; Gupta et al., 2013; Kim et al., 2009). Instead, they suggest that microfinance programmes should be accompanied by comprehensive couples training (Gupta et al., 2013).

Direct transfers of cash, food or food stamps: Nationwide governmental interventions or smaller scale non-governmental interventions, sometimes combined with nutrition training sessions; conditioned transfers for school attendance, vaccination etc. Among the programs implemented after 2014 that particularly stand out are a conditional cash transfer for schooling in South Africa (Pettifor et al., 2018), World Food Program in Ecuador (Hidrobo et al., 2016) and a cash transfer and nutrition discussion in Bangladesh (Roy et al., 2018).

> Main findings: In LMICs, interventions based on increased access to microfinance and assets are found to improve, but in some cases, they also worsen women's risk of violence. What seems to make a difference among them is the context in which women live. However, the evidence of the effectiveness

of such strategies is scarce and mixed when it comes to the sustainability of economic intervention impact. There is also a lack of evidence on whether direct targeting of women attains better results than targeting the head of the household (Kerr-Wilson et al., 2020)

3.1.2 Secondary Prevention Interventions

Secondary prevention involves the health and justice sector. It refers to both mitigating the immediate consequences of abuse by providing already-abused women and girls with services and supports (e.g. emergency contraception, post-exposure prophylactic-PEP, psychosocial support, and counselling), and also preventing recurrent or repeat abuse (e.g. through timely protection and safety for domestic violence survivors, removal of perpetrators from the household, and orders of protection) (Fergus, 2012).

Secondary prevention interventions usually require an **individual-level approach** and are thus more prevalent in **high-income countries**. Among the various strategies within this category, the only approach that has garnered promising results is "victim advocacy". This approach consists of support in the case management, connecting the victim to legal services, providing necessary information, and other victim advocacy services. In the high-income context, women-centred programs for survivors and perpetrator programs have conflicting evidence. Other approaches in this category (shelters, one-stop crisis centres, women's police stations and ICT services such as emergency hotlines and mobile applications) either do not have applicable data or have insufficient evidence.

There is insufficient data on the efficiency of all approaches in the secondary prevention category in **low- and middle-income countries**. So, the following paragraphs list the three most prevalent programmes (batterer intervention programs, screening and survivor services) conducted in **high-income countries** and their main findings.

Batterer intervention programs (BIP): Two systematic and one comprehensive reviews analysed the effects of court-mandated BIP in high-income settings. BIPs typically involve group education lasting from 8 to 24 weeks. One of the most well-known approaches is the "Duluth Model," a feminist approach that engages men in discussions about power and control. Other commonly used approaches are cognitive behavioural therapy (CBT) and anger management, both of which seek to change violent behaviour using established behavioural strategies, as well as discussions of thought patterns and beliefs (Smedslund et al., 2007). A few programmes tested new approaches, such as combining batterers' treatment with substance abuse programmes or applying racially and culturally adapted programs for specific groups.

<u>Main findings</u>: Although the authors of reviews on this type of intervention acknowledge the need for additional research, the meta-analysis conducted by Feder et al. (2008) does not provide strong support for the effectiveness of BIPs in reducing violence recidivism among perpetrators. Overall, batterers' programs have very high dropout rates, and there are few consequences for not completing the program. Furthermore, BIP can have potentially harmful effects on victims, especially when the cost of the court-mandated intervention is not subsidised.

The screening occurs through health services and involves pregnant women screened for violence during prenatal care. In situations of violence, health care providers can refer women to shelters, counselling or legal services. However, significant disagreement remains regarding the use of universal (which requires more time and resources) versus targeted screening.

> Main findings: Evaluations of screening programs have found statistically-significant positive results for identifying survivors of IPV, but there is no evidence whether it was followed by increased referrals to support agencies. According to the reviews, screening itself was not harmful to women. The few screening evaluations that actually reported decreases in violence usually combined screening with psychosocial support or another type of survivor service. Several screening evaluations report positive outcomes for women and their children, such as decreased depression, lower stress, and greater knowledge and use of services.

Survivor services: "women-centred" programmes targeting known survivors or women newly identified through the screening. These interventions use a combination of strategies to provide women with resources to reduce their future risk of violence and improve their health status. Survivors' services include two types of interventions: psychosocial counselling and advocacy interventions:

> *Psychosocial counselling*: may provide danger assessments, safety planning, and referrals to specialised services.

> Main findings: A successful screening program in Hong Kong provided pregnant women with an "empowerment intervention" (consisting of advice in the area of safety, decision making, problem-solving, and an "empathic understanding" component derived from client-centred therapy).

Advocacy interventions include many of the same components as the psychosocial and home visitation programs. These programs provide additional support to women from a layperson/community trained in identifying and accessing services.

<u>Main findings</u>: An intensive community-based advocacy intervention for women leaving a battered women's shelter in Michigan trained lay advocates to help women access the community resources they needed to reduce their risk of future IPV. Women who worked with advocates over two years experienced significantly less violence (p=0.03), reported a higher quality of life and social support and had less difficulty obtaining community resources than women not receiving such services.

3.2 Child abuse or maltreatment (CAM)

Child abuse or maltreatment constitutes all forms of physical or emotional ill-treatment, sexual abuse, neglect, negligent treatment, and commercial and other exploitation, resulting in actual or potential harm to the child's health, survival, development or dignity in the context of a relationship of responsibility, trust or power (WHO, 1999).

3.2.1 High-income countries

A recent meta-analysis conducted by the researchers from the University of Amsterdam (Put et al., 2017) provides a significant summary of findings on the effects of interventions for child maltreatment based on a relatively large analysed corpus (121 independent studies). The scope of this meta-analysis is global, yet the vast majority of included studies address CAM in the high-income contexts (USA, Europe, Canada, Australia and New Zealand). The study distinguishes between:

1. *Preventive interventions*, targeting the general population or targeting families at risk for child maltreatment, and
2. *Curative interventions*, targeting maltreating families aimed at reducing maltreatment or recurrence of maltreatment.

Analysed interventions mostly involved cognitive behavioural therapy, home visitation, parent training, family-based/multisystemic, substance abuse, and combined interventions effectively prevented or reduced child maltreatment. Delivery techniques used to engage parents included modelling, discussions, role-playing, monitoring, psycho-education, homework assignments, cognitive skills training and family group conferencing.

<u>Main findings</u>:

Preventive interventions: The types of preventive interventions that were effective in preventing child maltreatment were: home visitation interventions (d=.210), parent training interventions (d=.428), family-based/ multisystemic interventions (d=.343), substance abuse interventions (d=1.852) and combined interventions (d=.174). Before-school interventions (d=.148), general prevention interventions (d=.024), and crisis interventions (d=.407) did not have a significant effect on preventing child maltreatment.

Curative interventions: Types of curative interventions that were effective in reducing child maltreatment were home visitation interventions (d=.344), parent training interventions (d=.415), family-based/multisystemic interventions (d=0.346), substance abuse interventions (d=.385; trend significant), and cognitive behavioural therapy (d=.445). Crisis interventions (d=.335) did not significantly reduce child maltreatment, probably due to a lack of power (Put et al., 2017, p. 178).

The seemingly paradoxical result shows that *preventive interventions* with a short duration (up to 6 months) were more effective than preventive interventions of a longer duration. In contrast, no significant effect of intervention duration was found for curative interventions. (*Ibid*, p. 192). Effect sizes of preventive interventions increased as follow-up duration increased, possibly indicating the so-called "sleeper effect" *"(i.e. a delayed impact on the programme recipient)* of such interventions. For *curative interventions*, larger effect sizes were found for interventions focusing on improving parenting skills and those providing social or emotional support.

For *preventive interventions*, larger effect sizes were found for interventions focusing on increasing parents' self-confidence. For *curative interventions*, larger effect sizes were found for interventions that improve parenting skills, improve parents' personal skills, address parents' mental health problems, provide social or emotional support, and improve a child's well-being (*Ibid*, p. 193).

3.2.2 Middle- and low-income countries

Some traditional practices involve "[an] act or series of acts of commission or omission by a parent or other caregiver that results in harm to a child", which is a definition of child maltreatment formulated by the Centers for Disease Control and Prevention (CDC). Such practices can include female genital mutilation/cutting and child marriage. Impact evaluations indicate that transforming strong norms supporting these practices requires careful communication and the use of community dialogue and participation, as well as the involvement of multiple sectors and community stakeholders (Arango et al., 2014). Interventions include community mobilisation, group training for women and girls, cash transfers, and alternative "rites of passage".

There is an overall scarcity of robust empirical evidence on the effectiveness of interventions in this area. Most impact evaluations focused on changes in attitudes towards the practice itself. In contrast, significantly few measured actual changes in instances of victimisation or perpetration of harmful traditional practices or showed the empirical data that would allow for estimation of any kind of effect size. The reviewers especially emphasise the need to measure potential negative consequences of such harmful traditional practices interventions, based on their findings that unintended consequences could occur. These are, for example, the increased misconception that female genital mutilation/cutting (FGM/C) is acceptable if performed as a medically safe procedure.

> Main findings: The impact evaluation review shows that the community mobilisation programme TOSTAN conducted in Senegal significantly reduced the prevalence of FGM/C practices in participating rural villages. An important aspect of the programme is that villagers themselves identify priority issues for community action, among which FGM/C and IPV were singled out as critical problems. A quasi-experimental evaluation of the programme showed a significant reduction in VAWG and instances of FGM/C practices.
>
> Group training for women and girls, sometimes used in the harmful traditional practices interventions, has mixed results. The programmes that showed significant decreases in child marriages used a comprehensive set of activities, including intensive "life skills" training for unmarried girls, community

discussions, mentorship, community service activities to encourage parents to keep girls in school, economic incentives, etc. (Lee-Rife et al., 2012).

There is insufficient evidence of the effectiveness of approaches based on the organisation of alternative "rites of passage" ceremonies (training for girls in life skills culminating in a ceremony without female genital mutilation) in the LMIC context. In high-income countries, they are rarely applicable due to a lack of such practices in these contexts.

3.3 Child Sexual Abuse (CSA)

UNICEF's statistical analysis of violence against children estimates that, worldwide, around 120 million girls under the age of 20 (about 1 in 10) have experienced forced sexual intercourse or other forced sexual acts (UNICEF 2014). Child sexual abuse is a gendered crime; girls typically report lifetime rates three times higher than boys. Children are most likely to be sexually abused by a person known to them, usually an adult or older child who is a family member, relative, family friend or in a relationship of trust or authority (Pinheiro 2006).

UNICEF's impact evaluation study (Radford et al., 2015) assessed interventions to prevent and respond to child sexual abuse and exploitation in all sectors from the national/government level to health, criminal justice, education, child protection, and community and civil society.

Main findings: There are significant gaps in the evidence, but plenty of examples show promising results.

National child protection system-building responses (including legislative reform; strategy development and planning; mapping needs and gaps in services; capacity building etc.): due to the overlap between VAWG and child sexual abuse, coordinated governmental responses are required, along with multi-agency/cross-sector collaboration, community engagement and monitoring.

Prevention: in HICs, prevention strategies focus more on child sexual abuse. In LMICs, more attention has been given to child sexual exploitation, AIDS prevention and gender-based intimate partner violence. However, there is a lack of good, robust evidence for prevention measures that reduce sexual abuse and exploitation rates.

Identification and protection: Health workers play a crucial role in identifying sexually exploited and abused children, and training on indicators of sexual abuse have been provided in HICs and LMICs, especially in connection with sexually transmitted infection (STI)/HIV services. Child protection services in HICs have been the primary agencies responsible for protecting children from sexual abuse and exploitation. The general trend in HICs has been to provide family support and earlier interventions. Child protection in LMICs is more commonly provided through non-governmental organisations (NGOs) and community groups. There is as yet no clear evidence about their effectiveness in helping to identify and refer children and adolescents at risk of sexual abuse and exploitation (Wessells 2009). There has been an increase in the prosecution of sex offenders in some HICs, particularly for online abuse, while prosecution rates in LMICS remain low.

Recovery and integration: Robust research and evaluation in this area are seriously lacking, particularly in LMICs. HICs have focused more on psychological recovery for sexually abused children, while reintegration of victims has had greater attention in LMICs. Trauma-Focused

Cognitive Behavioural Therapy is the only intervention with any robust evidence of effectiveness.

3.4 Elder abuse

It is estimated that elder abuse affects almost one in six (more than 140 million) older people. Yet, despite this staggering fact, elder abuse is a neglected global public health priority, especially compared with other types of violence. For example, none of the 169 targets of the UN's recently adopted 17 Sustainable Development Goals explicitly addresses violence against older people.

The prevalence of elder abuse within families has been notoriously difficult to assess. That is due to restricted access to older adults, who are often in very fragile states (advanced age, deteriorating physical and psychological health). They are also often dependent on their family members/caregivers and sometimes unaware or unwilling to admit to being victims of violence perpetrated by their close ones. Furthermore, country-specific and culture-specific social norms – such as filial piety and the existence of elder caregiving policies – contribute to wide variations in prevalence between WHO regional estimates. Only a few systematic reviews on the global prevalence of elder abuse exist for these reasons. The review conducted by the researchers from the University of Southern California (Yon et al., 2017) is the first meta-analysis in elder abuse studies.

One of the limiting factors in this meta-analysis is that most of the scientific literature comes from high-income countries (from 52 selected studies, 47 studies refer to high-income or upper-middle-income countries). Therefore, if more studies from low-income and middle-income countries were available, the current findings might not hold entirely. Thus, a complimentary, integrative review conducted by the researchers from two Brazilian universities includes studies from

Latin America (mainly Brazil), Portugal and the USA (Ribeiro et al., 2021).

> Main findings: Prevalence estimates for abuse subtypes were highest for psychological abuse, followed by financial abuse, neglect, physical abuse, and sexual abuse. Significant associations were found between overall prevalence estimates and sample size, income classification, and data collection method. However, the research found no significant difference in prevalence between older women and men (Yon et al., 2017). The Brazilian study finds the following: that elder abuse is mainly committed by family members (children, spouse, grandchildren, etc.), that it is twice as likely to affect older adult people living alone or with a family member than those living in extended care facilities and assisted by formal caregivers, and that, besides the advanced age, family disfunction was the second major predictor of violence (Ribeiro et al., 2021).

4. Gaps and limitations in available empirical evidence

A more thorough discussion of the limitations and gaps in the empirical evidence on the effectiveness of VAWG programmes presented in Landscaping report 3 (*Violence Against Women and Girls: Effectiveness of Intervention programs*) would generally apply in the case of research on domestic violence. That is not surprising, given that both VAWG and DV research fields are predominantly based on the research on IPV intervention programmes.

Measuring the effectiveness of DV interventions is especially difficult due to the very intimate and emotionally loaded character of the situation, a complex interplay of social norms, individual attitudes and community customs and beliefs. Proper understanding of this complex interplay is not only important for choosing and delivering an effective intervention but also for organising a methodologically sound and rigorous evaluation design.

Limited quantity of empirical evidence

Maybe as a consequence of this intrinsic difficulty of the topic, there is, in general, relatively little solid empirical evidence on the effectiveness of DV intervention programmes. However, the evidence base is fastly improving over the last decades. Moreover, there are entire domains of domestic violence (e.g., violence against older people, against the parents, or persons with disabilities) which are researched with only a few evaluation studies. That has led most authors of systematic reviews and meta-analyses to resort to qualitative "narrative summaries" of the available evidence on programme effectiveness rather than more robust quantitative meta-analytic techniques. However, the scarcity of solid empirical evidence is not only due to the overall lack of DV interventions. It is even more so due to the lack of robust impact assessment studies in the applied interventions. In fact, in most systematic reviews, the number of intervention programmes with solid evaluation designs was a small fraction of all DV interventions.

A good illustration of the scarcity of the DV intervention studies with robust evaluation design can be found in Picon and colleagues (2017) systematic review of the IPV interventions. The authors started their search with 48,788 identified studies and ended up with 45 impact evaluation studies that have fulfilled their inclusion criteria (**Figure 7**).

Figure 7: Selection of impact evaluation studies in Picon et al. (2017)

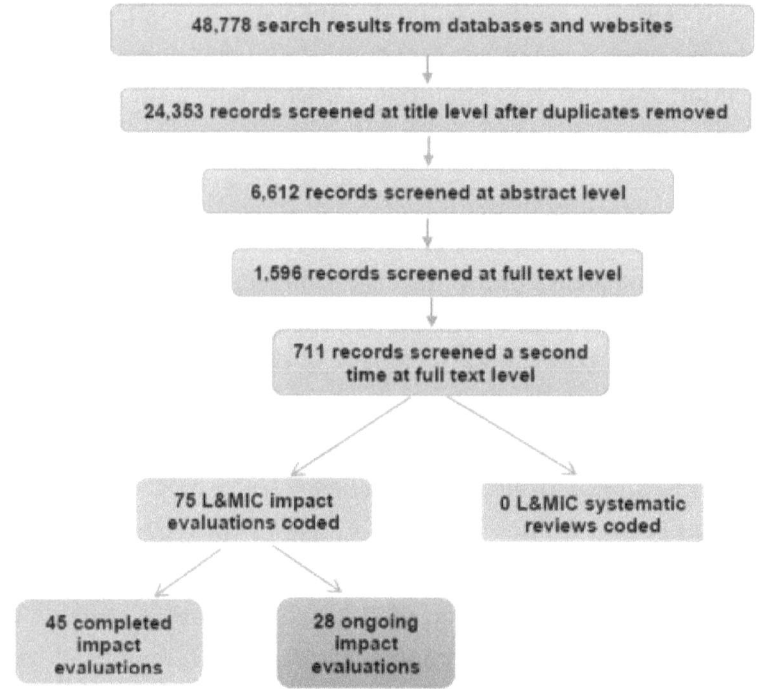

Source: Picon et al. (2017). Intimate partner violence prevention: An evidence gap map.

Limited quality of empirical evidence

The numerous quality issues further limit even the little empirical evidence on the DV effectiveness. For example, reviewed studies have generally relied on single-factor solutions, offered a poor general understanding of the mechanism of targeted change, and have limited consistency, rigour, and quality of employed evaluation processes, measures and methodologies (Ellsberg et al., 2014; Florquin, 2016; Picon et al., 2017; Bott, Morrison, & Ellsberg, 2005). Furthermore, although there is an increasing effort to evaluate programmes' impact, the teams conducting interventions, unfortunately, tend to lack the skills, funding and expertise to generate robust empirical evidence (Heise, 2011, Ellsberg et al., 2014).

The meta-analysis of Pundir and colleagues (2020) in the domain of IPV interventions illustrates the heterogeneity in the quality of identified impact assessment studies, with the majority of the identified impact assessment studies evaluated to be of "medium" or "low" confidence (**Figure 8**).

*Figure 8: **Number of systematic reviews by study confidence***

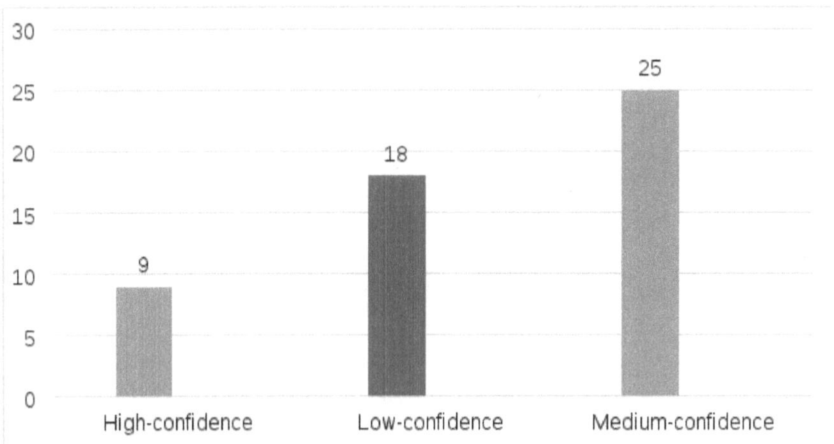

Source: Pundir P, Saran A, White H, Subrahmanian R, Adona J. (2020).

There are many quality issues in the studies evaluating DV interventions identified by various authors. Some of the main ones are the following:

- Risk of bias due to not employing complete experimental protocols
- Lack of methodological rigour & high variability in the quality of impact assessment
- Small target groups (Lack of statistical power)
- Lack of standardised measures of DV outcomes
- Lack of process monitoring and evaluation
- Lack of direct measurement of behavioural impact
- Inconsistent implementation of standard evaluation research

protocols

Gaps in the scope of empirical evidence

Limitations in the quantity and quality of the available empirical evidence on the effectiveness of DV interventions mean that there are still many critical empirical gaps. These gaps constrain the development of effective intervention programmes and, thus, general reduction of DV incidence. The main empirical gaps in the area of DV interventions are:

Limited evidence from the LMIC context

Empirical research on the effectiveness of DV interventions is much more limited in terms of sheer numbers and tends to be less robust.

Unequal evidence across forms of domestic violence

The majority of DV programmes focus on (some form of) intimate partner violence, with much less attention directed towards other forms of domestic violence, such as violence towards the elderly, children, persons with disabilities, etc.

Unequal evidence across different intervention types

Some intervention approaches, such as micro-finance or relationship-level approaches, are more common and better researched.

Little evidence on vulnerable groups and intersectoral approach

Another imbalance in the available evidence is related to the fact that most of the assessed DV interventions were conducted focusing on broader population groups of women, men and children, with little or no regard to the intersectionality of various disadvantages.

Limited evidence from conflict and severely deprived areas

Very little usable empirical evidence on DV intervention effectiveness comes from severely deprived or conflict areas.

Lack of generalisability to broader population(s)

Very few evaluations assessed the impact on DV at the broader community or population levels.

Lack of scalability to other contexts

Most of the programmes exclusively focus on the impact of their intervention in a given context and for a given respondent group, offering little consideration to the potential generalisability of their findings across different settings.

Lack of interventions targeting institutional change

Most DV interventions focus on individuals, groups, or communities, with only a few evaluating programmes targeting formal and informal institutional changes.

Lack of assessment of intervention intensity

Most evaluation studies do not investigate the relationship between different programme intensities and their target outcomes, thus losing the ability to identify the optimal intervention intensity.

Lack of long-term impact assessments

Most studies measure only short-term outcomes, either right after the intervention or within six months, even though most interventions have long-term rather than short-term objectives.

Lack of knowledge of the mechanism in which intervention works

There is relatively little consideration and solid evidence on the intervention mechanism and how desired change is generated and sustained. Likewise, widespread "conflicting" evidence among the programmes implementing similar strategies suggests poorly understood change pathways.

Lack of studies examining the cost-effectiveness

Cost-effectiveness is rarely examined, leading to limited knowledge of how to use often scarce resources, especially in LMICs.

Other limitations of the impact assessment studies

Apart from their limited quantity and impaired quality, impact assessment studies have a few additional methodological constraints that should be considered when interpreting their findings.

Selection bias

Given that most DV interventions are implemented without or with only limited impact evaluation (see **Figure 7**), the question remains what the impact of unevaluated studies is and whether it differs from that of the evaluated ones. In other words, one cannot simply assume that the studies that happened to be evaluated are a representative sample of all DV interventions. And, if they indeed differ from the rest of DV programmes (i.e. if there is a selection bias), how are they different? One plausible answer to this question is that the studies whose impact is measured are also programmes that were planned and executed more rigorously, have more resources available, and have other favourable characteristics that made them more likely to be successful in their objectives.

Publication bias

Furthermore, given that the evidence on the effectiveness of DV interventions comes from the published reports, most of which were peer-reviewed, it is also likely that they contain a certain amount of publication bias. In other words, there are more positive outcomes reported in these because it is harder to publish a study with no impact. Unfortunately, given this field's general infancy, there are currently no available studies examining possible selection or publication biases. Thus, it is impossible to estimate their degree and consequences on empirical findings. So, one should consider these methodological risks when interpreting available empirical evidence.

The fragility of statistical significance

Where quantitative estimates of effect sizes of DV intervention programmes are available, one should be aware of the inherent limitations of the statistical significance as the criteria. Therefore, their interpretation should not be made "blindly" and overemphasised. Instead, they should be interpreted within a broader set of methodological considerations, such as available sample size and statistical power, empirical design, reliability and validity of indicator measures, the potential influence of various unaccounted confounding or spurious factors etc. Thus, a programme without statistically significant outcomes is not necessarily an unsuccessful programme and vice versa.

Summary

Domestic violence (DV) is a widespread form of abuse worldwide. Globally, the victims of domestic violence are overwhelmingly women, and women tend to experience more severe forms of violence. It is assumed that domestic violence is one of the most underreported crimes for both women and men. Over a quarter of married/partnered women aged 15 years or older have been subjected to physical and/or sexual violence from a current or former husband or intimate male partner at least once in their lifetime (WHO, 2018). Likewise, it is estimated that elder abuse affects almost one in six (more than 140 million) older people. There is a strong relationship between the level of gender equality in a given country and the incidence of domestic violence in the country, with less domestic violence occurring in countries with a higher level of gender equality.

Domestic violence was a long-overlooked and ignored policy issue despite its high prevalence. However, in recent decades, increased attention has been placed on various forms of domestic violence, including its most prevalent forms of intimate partner violence (IPV) and child abuse. The expanded policy focus has led to the global growth of the DV intervention programmes of various forms, scopes and target types of violence.

In this report, we aim to present and evaluate existing empirical evidence on the effectiveness of interventions in the field of domestic violence gathered around the world so far. In other words, we will try to answer "what works", i.e., what is known to be an effective intervention strategy, under which conditions, and for which outcomes. Such evidence could then be used in designing future DV interventions by avoiding identified inefficiencies and building upon observed effective aspects of these programmes.

The report is based on the literature review and summarises the findings presented in various systematic reviews and meta-analyses published over the last decade. We prioritised compiling evidence from rigorous empirical studies using experimental (i.e. randomised controlled trials – RCTs) and quasi-experimental designs. The evidence comprises studies on intimate partner violence, child abuse and maltreatment (including harmful traditional practices), child sexual abuse and elderly abuse. Other types of domestic abuse, such as abuse of pregnant women or abuse of persons with disabilities, are also reviewed where evidence is available. In the first chapter, we shortly discuss various forms of domestic and family violence, their prevalence, and their consequences.

In chapter two, we outline some of the critical characteristics of the DV interventions and their incidence. Main empirical findings on the effectiveness of DV interventions are discussed in chapter three, followed by the evaluation of limitations and gaps in presented evidence in chapter four.

Main findings

Strong growth of DV intervention programmes during the last decade

Programmes aiming to prevent domestic violence started in the late 20th century and rapidly evolved during the last decade. At the same time, an increasing number of these interventions have applied elaborate impact assessments, thus slowly building up the evidence database on their effectiveness.

The large diversity of forms of DV interventions

A variety of approaches have been used in domestic violence interventions. They differ across the type of violence they are focused on, the population group they target, the intervention strategy, the moment of intervention (i.e., primary vs secondary interventions), the location and geographical scope of the intervention (e.g., high-income vs LMIC contexts), etc. DV interventions are focused at the individual, group, community or system-wide levels. Common forms across these levels are one-on-one individual therapy or training sessions, work with couples and families, group-based training, community mobilisation efforts, or "gender transformative" programmes that aim to change system-wide settings. Most domestic violence interventions focus on primary or secondary prevention of IPV. But an increasing number of them are expanding their focus to the other forms of domestic violence. In particular, there is a small but growing number of programmes on domestic child abuse, elderly abuse, parental abuse, home care abuse,

abuse of persons with disabilities, abuse of pregnant women, abuse of LGBTI+ persons, etc.

Three groups of sources of evidence on DV intervention effectiveness

The DV interventions' growth and effectiveness necessitated compiling systematic reviews of available empirical evidence in this area. Over the recent years, several systematic overviews of such empirical evidence have been published, although none of them is exclusively and comprehensively focused on all forms of domestic violence. Furthermore, most of the available reviews focus on specific domains of evidence, either in terms of geographic regions, particular intervention strategies or particular forms of domestic violence. In general, we can divide the available literature on the effectiveness of DV intervention programmes into three groups. The first group of comprehensive reviews tackle all forms of violence against women and girls globally. Four such systematic reviews have been published in the last few years. The second group of sources consists of systematic reviews focused exclusively on particular forms of domestic violence, including individual reviews on IPV interventions, child abuse and elderly abuse. Finally, the third group of reviews consisted of meta-analyses focused on particular DV intervention approaches or target populations. These include, for example, meta-analyses of the effectiveness of the interventions on perpetrators of IPV, reviews of the impact of advocacy interventions against various forms of VAWG, or systematic reviews of interventions preventing DV against pregnant women.

A limited quantity of available empirical evidence on the effectiveness of DV interventions

Maybe as a consequence of the intrinsic difficulty of the research topic, there is, in general, relatively little solid empirical evidence on the effectiveness of DV intervention programmes. Moreover, there are entire domains of domestic violence (e.g., violence towards the elderly, against the parents, or persons with disabilities) that are researched with only a few evaluation studies. That has led most authors of systematic reviews and meta-analyses to resort to qualitative "narrative summaries" of the available evidence on programme effectiveness rather than more robust quantitative meta-analytic techniques. However, the scarcity of solid empirical evidence is not only due to the overall lack of DV interventions. It is even more so to the lack of robust impact assessment studies in the applied interventions. In fact, in most systematic reviews, the number of intervention programmes with solid evaluation designs was a small fraction of all DV interventions.

Positive change is possible

Examination of available empirical evidence shows that the desired reduction of incidences of various forms of DV across different settings and situations is possible. Indeed, several DV programmes have established empirical proof of the positive effects of their interventions.

High-income countries

Some primary prevention programmes have significantly reduced DV incidence rates in high-income countries. For example, an intervention conducted in four family-planning clinics in Northern California found a 71% decrease in the odds of pregnancy coercion among women in the intervention group compared to participants in the control clinics. Likewise, two Canadian programmes on "Healthy Relationships" (Wolfe et al., 2009) showed significant reductions in dating violence perpetration in the intervention group compared to the control groups.

In the case of child abuse interventions in the high-income contexts, the effective interventions focused on increasing parents' self-confidence and were delivered by professionals only. Effect sizes of preventive interventions increased as follow-up duration increased, possibly indicating the so-called "sleeper effect" of such interventions. For *curative interventions*, larger effect sizes were found for interventions focusing on improving parenting skills and those providing social or emotional support. The secondary interventions in the high-income countries with the victims of domestic violence have often shown success in enhancing survivors' physical and mental health. On the other hand, secondary prevention programmes with the perpetrators of IPV still offer limited effectiveness in reducing the rates of re-victimisation. There is also relatively limited success in prevention programmes to reduce revictimization incidences.

Low- and middle-income countries

In the LMIC context, the main focus of DV interventions is the primary prevention of various forms of domestic violence. Findings show that it is possible to reduce the prevalence of violence, with some interventions reaching substantial positive effects within the timeframe of the programmes. There is good evidence that well-designed, long-term, and more intensive interventions, primarily when also addressing alcohol abuse, effectively reduce women's experiences of IPV. Examples are the Indashyikirwa programme in Rwanda (Dunkle et al., 2019) and the VATU programme in Zambia (Murray et al., 2019). Recent good examples of effective community mobilisation projects: Transforming Masculinities in DRC (Le Roux et al., 2019), Rural Response System in Ghana (Ogum-Alangea et al., 2019). To effectively reduce IPV, these interventions need a strong design and implementation and multi-year intensive community mobilisation (Kerr-Wilson, 2020).

In the case of child abuse, particularly concerning various harmful traditional practices, impact evaluation reviews show that the community mobilisation programmes offer a potentially effective approach. For example, the TOSTAN programme conducted in Senegal significantly reduced the prevalence of female genital mutilation/cutting practices in participating rural villages. A significant aspect of the programme is that villagers themselves identify priority issues for community action, among which female genital mutilation/cutting and IPV were singled out as critical problems.

Most of the interventions have limited or no impact

Despite the several effective DV programmes, many interventions are ineffective in reaching their primary goals, with little usable accompanying evidence that could be used to determine factors and barriers that were impairing its effects. For example, of all DV interventions using an experimental or quasi-experimental study design and summarized in one of the most rigorous systematic reviews in the field (Arango et al., 2014), more than two-thirds (67%) had no recorded impact on the targeted DV outcomes. Conversely, around one in eight reviewed studies had an evident significant positive effect. An additional 15% of studies had a positive but 'mixed' effect, indicating that obtained findings were positive on some, but not all, measured outcomes. Finally, in around 4% of assessed interventions, the impact was assessed as significantly negative or identified significant adverse outcomes.

Unintended consequences are a rare but persistent threat

Some programmes evidently lead to unintended consequences for their participants or broader target populations. Although the proportion is relatively small, it is still a reason for concern and additional caution and risk assessment in designing and implementing future DV programmes. For example, it is shown that microfinance/economic empowerment programmes alone do not suffice to decrease IPV-related rates and may increase controlling behaviours (Green et al., 2015; Gupta et al., 2013; Kim et al., 2009). Such findings also illustrate the importance of integrating and conducting a careful impact assessment study of any DV intervention to examine its effectiveness and avoid harming or, especially, repeating the same mistakes.

Overall, most of the answers are still unanswered – evidence gaps are abundant

Despite the growing evidence base, the fact that few DV interventions are implementing rigorous impact assessment studies and that even fewer among these are effective means that the field is still primarily characterised by the abundance of evidence gaps. These include:

- There is much less robust empirical research on the effectiveness of DV interventions coming from LMIC contexts.
- There is a considerable difference in the number of studies across different research areas.
- Some areas, such as micro-finance interventions, receive much more attention than complex programmes to transform system-level discrimination or change social norms.
- Limited evidence exists on the effectiveness of intervention programmes with particularly vulnerable groups of women and girls, such as the elderly, LGBT populations, people living with disabilities, chronic illness, people belonging to various ethnic or religious minorities, etc.
- There is little empirical evidence on DV intervention effectiveness in deprived or conflict regions.
- Very few evaluations assessed the impact on DV beyond their respondent groups, at the broader community or population levels.
- We know very little or, in many cases, nothing regarding the medium- to the long-term effectiveness of various DV programmes.
- Few interventions examine the mechanism of change or the influence of related risk factors, resulting in little usable knowledge on this crucial question.
- Very few studies examined the cost-effectiveness or the optimal intensity of their interventions concerning the desired

outcomes.

Relatively poor quality of available empirical evidence

Apart from the limited quantity, there are many severe methodological flaws in the accumulated empirical evidence. The quality of evidence collected in reviewed studies is impaired due to their limited methodological consistency, rigour, quality of employed evaluation standards and processes, assessment methods and research methodologies. Conducted impact assessment studies were often based on a poor general understanding of the impact mechanism, targeted outcomes and various moderating and risk factors in the intervention process. Furthermore, impact assessments were often conducted with small sample sizes and inappropriate and unreliable outcome measures, with no effective control of the influence of potential confounding factors. Furthermore, almost all evaluated programmes measured only short-term outcomes, thus failing to provide information on the medium to long-term outcomes, even though these were usually their primary programme objectives. As a result of these quality issues, even the observed positive effects of some of the DV policy interventions have to be interpreted carefully, requiring repeated empirical confirmation across different contexts and over a more extended period. These limitations also point out the need for significant improvements in the impact assessment approaches in the DV programmes, which will require more internal team resources and programme funding for this crucial aspect of programme implementations.

There is insufficient evidence for scaling up good practices

The limited amount of empirical evidence, various quality issues limiting its validity and the limited number of studies with identified positive outcomes restrict accumulation and scaling up the evidence base. The fact that few impact assessment studies examine their effects across broader population groups or different contexts further prevents their findings' generalisability. Moreover, the entire field is still characterised by little understanding of the processes and mechanisms of interventions to achieve their desired changes. Also, as a relatively recent field of research, there is an excellent variety of intervention approaches and impact assessment designs, with considerable heterogeneity of used outcomes and their measures. These factors further prevent comparability of the results across DV programmes and extrapolation of some empirical insights that could inform new interventions. Such a situation also leads to many "conflicting" results, where effects across the similar interventions on the same outcome are opposing or inconsistent and where effects on various outcomes within the same study are both positive and negative.

Future directions

In general, the review of the state of available empirical evidence in this area shows that it is still in its infancy and urgent need of more investment into building better research infrastructure. Collection of more robust empirical evidence is especially needed in those areas where the gaps are currently the biggest, e.g., in the conflict areas, in cases of intersectoral vulnerabilities, in LMIC contexts. Furthermore, impact evaluation of DV programmes has to start implementing a stricter design to avoid various quality issues and offer clear and valid evaluations of their impact. DV programmes should also be able to provide evidence on the potential scope and limitations of their scalability regarding both potential target populations and social contexts. Related to the issue of their scalability is also the issue of their cost-effectiveness, which deserves much more attention in future DV programmes and their impact assessments. Such considerations would greatly contribute to the better allocation of available resources and general improvement in the accountability and effectiveness of DV programmes.

References:

Arango, D. & Morton, M. & Gennari, F. & Kiplesund, S. & Ellsberg, M. (2014). Interventions to prevent or reduce violence against women and girls: A systematic review of reviews. Washington DC: The World Bank, DOI:http://dx.doi.org/10.13140/RG.2.1.2545.6168

Austrian, A. & Muthengi, M. (2013). Safe and smart savings products for vulnerable adolescent girls in Kenya and Uganda. New York: Population Council.

Bandiera, O. & Buehren, N. & Burgess, R. & Goldstein, M. & Gulesci, S. & Rasul, I. & Sulaiman, M. (2018). Women's Empowerment in Action: Evidence from a Randomized Control Trial in Africa. Washington, DC: The World Bank.

Bott, S., Morrison, A., & Ellsberg, M. (2005). Preventing and responding to gender-based violence in middle and low-income countries: A global review and analysis. Working Paper. Washington DC: The World Bank, DOI:10.1596/1813-9450-3618[3]

Breiding, M. et al. (2015). Intimate Partner Violence Surveillance: Uniform Definitions and Recommended Data Elements. Atlanta: Center for Disease Control and Prevention.

Coker, A.L. & Bush, H.M. & Cook-Craig, P.G. & DeGue, S.A. & Clear, E.R. & Brancato, C.J. ... & Recktenwald, E.A. (2017). RCT testing bystander effectiveness to reduce

---

violence. American Journal of Preventive Medicine, 52(5), 566-578.

Cork, C. & White, R.G. & Noel, P. & Bergin, N. (2018). Randomised controlled trials of interventions addressing intimate partner violence in sub-Saharan Africa: A systematic review. Trauma, Violence & Abuse https://doi.org/10.1177/1524838018784585

Doyle, K. & Levtov, R. G. & Barker, G. & Bastian, G. G. & Bingenheimer, J. B. & Kazimbaya, S., ... & Shattuck, D. (2018). Gender-transformative Bandebereho couples' intervention to promote male engagement in reproductive and maternal health and violence prevention in Rwanda: Findings from a randomized controlled trial. PloS One, 13(4).

Duggan, A. & McFarlane, E. C. & Windham, A. M. & Rohde, C. A. & Salkever, D. S. & Fuddy, L. (1999). Evaluation of Hawaii's healthy start program. The Future of Children, 3(1): 66-90.

Dunkle et al. (2019). Impact of the Indashyikriwa training curriculum for couples on intimate partner violence in Rwanda: cluster randomized control trial. Draft manuscript – What Works.

Ellsberg, M. & Arango, D. & Morton, M. & Gennari, F. & Kiplesund, S. & Contreras, M. & Watts, C. (2014). Prevention of Violence against Women and Girls: What Does the Evidence Say?. The Lancet. http://dx.doi.org/10.1016/S0140-6736(14)61703-7

Esquivel-Santoveña, Esteban & Lambert, Teri & Hamel, John. (2013). Partner Abuse Worldwide. Partner Abuse. 4. 6-75. 10.1891/1946-6560.4.1.e14.

Feder, L. & Austin, S. & Wilson, D. (2008). Court Mandated Interventions for Individuals Convicted of Domestic Violence. Campbell Systematic Review (12).

Fergus, L. (2012). Background paper for the UN Women Expert Group Meeting: Prevention of Violence Against Women and Girls in Bangkok, Thailand. Bangkok, Thailand: UN Women.

Florquin, Nicolas, (2016). Gender-Based Violence Interventions: Opportunities for Innovation. https://www.researchgate.net/publication/335335870_ Gender-Based_Violence_Interventions_ Opportunities_for_Innovation

Fulu, Emma, Kerr-Wilson, Alice, et al. (2015). What works to prevent violence against women and girls evidence reviews. Paper 2: Interventions to prevent violence against women and girls. What Works to Prevent Violence Against Women and Girls Global Programme, Pretoria, South Africa.

Green, E. P. & Blattman, C.& Jamison, J. & Annan, J. (2015). Women's entrepreneurship and intimate partner violence: A cluster randomized trial of microenterprise assistance and partner participation in post-conflict Uganda. Social Science & Medicine, 133, 177-188.

Gupta, J. & Falb, K. L. & Lehmann, H. & Kpebo, D. & Xuan, Z. & Hossain, M., ... & Annan, J. (2013). Gender norms and economic empowerment intervention to reduce intimate partner violence against women in rural Côte d'Ivoire: A randomized controlled pilot study. BMC International Health & Human Rights, 13(1), 46.

Heise, Lori, (2011). What works to prevent partner violence? An evidence overview. Working Paper. STRIVE Research Consortium, London School of Hygiene and Tropical Medicine, London.

Hester, Marianne & Westmarland, Nicole. (2005). Tackling Domestic Violence: Effective Interventions and Approaches.

Hidrobo, M. & Peterman, A. & Heise, L. (2016). The effect of cash, vouchers, and food transfers on intimate partner violence: Evidence from a randomized experiment in Northern Ecuador. American Economic Journal: Applied Economics, 8(3), 284-303.

Hossain, M. & Zimmerman, C. & Kiss, L. & Abramsky, T. & Kone, D., ... & Watts, C. (2014). Working with men to prevent intimate partner violence in a conflict-affected setting: a pilot cluster randomized controlled trial in rural Côte d'Ivoire. BMC Public Health, 14(1), 339-350.

IRC. (2012). Getting down to business: Women's economic and social empowerment in Burundi. New York: International Rescue Committee.

Jahanfar, S., Howard, L.M., Medley, N. (2014). Interventions for preventing or reducing domestic violence against pregnant women. Cochrane Database of Systematic Reviews 2014, Issue 11. Art. No.: CD009414. DOI: 10.1002/14651858.CD009414.pub3.

Jewkes, R. & Nduna, M. & Levin, J. & Jama, N. & Dunkle, K. & Puren, A. & Duvvury, N. (2008). Impact of stepping stones on incidence of HIV and HSV-2 and sexual behaviour in rural South Africa: Cluster randomised controlled trial. BMJ, 337, a506.

Karakurt G, Koç E, Çetinsaya EE, Ayluçtarhan Z, Bolen S. (2019). Meta-analysis and systematic review for the treatment of perpetrators of intimate partner violence. Neurosci Biobehav Rev. 105:220-230. doi: 10.1016/j.neubiorev.2019.08.006.

Kelly, L. and Westmarland, N. (2015) Domestic Violence Perpetrator Programmes: Steps Towards Change. Project Mirabal Final Report. London and Durham: London Metropolitan University and Durham University.

Kerr-Wilson, A. & Gibbs, A. & McAslan Fraser E. & Ramsoomar, L. & Parke, A. & Khuwaja, HMA. & Jewkes, R. (2020). A rigorous global evidence review of interventions to prevent violence against women and girls, What Works to Prevent Violence Against Women and Girls Global Programme, Pretoria, South Africa. https://www.whatworks.co.za/documents/ publications/ 374-evidence-reviewfweb/file

Kim, J. et al. (2009). Assessing the incremental effects of combining economic and health interventions: the IMAGE study in South Africa. WHO Bulletin, 87, 824-832.

Lee-Rife, S. & Malhotra, A. & Warner, A. & Glinksi, A. M. (2012). What Works to Prevent Child Marriage: A Review of the Evidence. Studies in Family Planning 43(4): 287-303.

Le Roux, E. & Corboz, J. & Scott, N. & Sandilands, M. & Baghuma Lele, U. & Bezzolato, E., Jewkes, R. (2019). Engaging with faith groups to prevent VAWG in conflict-affected communities: results from two community surveys in the DRC. Draft manuscript – What Works

Livingston, M. (2008). Recent trends in risky alcohol consumption and related harm among young people in Victoria, Australia. Public Health, Vol. 32, No. 3, https://doi.org/10.1111/j.1753-6405.2008.00227.x

Middlebrooks, J. S., & Audage, N. C. (2008). The effects of childhood stress on health across the lifespan. National Center for Injury Prevention and Control of the Centers for Disease Control and Prevention.

Miller, E., et al. (2012). "Coaching boys into men": a cluster-randomized controlled trial of a dating violence prevention program. Adolescent Health, 51(5), 431-438.

Murray et al. (2019). Effectiveness of the Common Elements Treatment Approach (CETA) in reducing intimate partner violence and hazardous alcohol use in Zambia (VATU): a randomised controlled trial. Draft manuscript - What Works

Ogum-Alangea, D., Addo-Lartey, A., Chirwa, E., Sikweyiya, Y., Coker-Appiah, D., Jewkes, R., & Adanu, R. (2019). The Rural Response System Intervention to reduce Intimate Partner Violence in the Central Region of Ghana: Findings from a cluster-randomized controlled trial evaluation. Draft manuscript – What Works.

Pettifor, A., Lippman, S. A., Gottert, A., Suchindran, C. M., Selin, A., ... & Tollman, S. (2018). Community mobilization to modify harmful gender norms and reduce HIV risk: Results from a community cluster randomized trial in South Africa. Journal of the International AIDS Society, 21(7).

Picon, MG, Rankin, K, Ludwig, J, Sabet, SM, Delaney, A and Holst, A. (2017). Intimate partner violence prevention: an evidence gap map, 3ie Evidence Gap Map Report 8. International Initiative for Impact Evaluation (3ie). https://www.researchgate.net/publication/ 324840313_Intimate_partner_violence_prevention _An_evidence_gap_map

Pinheiro, P.S. (2006). The United Nations Secretary-General's world's report on violence against children. United Nations: New York.

Pulerwitz, J., Hughes, L., Mehta, M., Kidanu, A., Verani, F., & Tewolde, S. (2015). Changing gender norms and reducing intimate partner violence: Results from a quasi-experimental intervention study with young men in Ethiopia. American Journal of Public Health, 105(1), 132-137.

Pundir P, Saran A, White H, Subrahmanian R, Adona J. (2020). Interventions for reducing violence against children in low- and middle-income countries: An evidence and gap map. Campbell Systematic Reviews, Vol. 16/4. https://doi.org/10.1002/cl2.1120

Put, Claudia & Assink, Mark & Boekhout, Noelle. (2017). Predicting child maltreatment: A meta-analysis of the predictive validity of risk assessment instruments. Child abuse & neglect. 73. 71-88. 10.1016/j.chiabu.2017.09.016.

Radford, L. & Allnock, D. & Hynes, P. (2015). Preventing and Responding to Child Sexual Abuse and Exploitation: Evidence review, New York: UNICEF

Ribeiro MN, Santo FH, Diniz CX, Araujo KB, Lisboa MG, Souza CR. (2021)Scientific evidence of the violence against the older adult: an integrative review. Acta Paul Enferm, DOI:http://dx.doi.org/10.37689/ actaape/2021AR00403

Rivas, C., Vigurs, C., Cameron, J., and Yeo, L. (2019). A realist review of which advocacy interventions work for which abused women under what circumstances. Cochrane Database of Systematic Reviews 2019, Issue 6. Art. No.: CD013135. DOI: 10.1002/14651858.CD013135.pub2.

Roy, S., Hidrobo, M., Hoddinott, J., & Ahmed, A. (2018). Transfers, behavior change communication, and intimate partner violence: Post-program evidence from rural Bangladesh. Review of Economics and Statistics, 1(0), 1-45.

Smedslund, G., Dalsbø, T. K., Sterio, A. K., Winsvold, A., & Clench-Aas, J. (2007).Cognitive behavioral therapy for men who physically abuse their female partner. Cochrane Database of Systematic Reviews (2).

UNICEF, (2014). Hidden in Plain Sight: A statistical analysis of violence against children. New York: UNICEF

Verma, R., et al. (2008). Promoting gender equity as a strategy to reduce HIV risk and gender-based violence among young men in India, in Horizons Final Report. Washington: Population Council.

Wessels M. (2009). Do no harm: toward contextually appropriate psychosocial support in international emergencies. American Psychologist, 64(8):842–854.

Wolfe, D. et al. (2009). A school-based program to prevent adolescent dating violence: A cluster randomized trial. Archives of Pediatrics & Adolescent Medicine, 163(8), 692–699.

World Health Organization, (1999). Report of the Consultation on Child Abuse Prevention. Geneva: World Health Organization.

World Health Organization, (2002). The Toronto Declaration on the Global Prevention of Elder Abuse. Geneva: World Health Organization

World Health Organization, (2005). WHO multi-country study on women's health and domestic violence against women. Geneva: World Health Organization.

World Health Organization, (2013). Global and regional estimates of violence against women: prevalence and health effects of intimate partner violence and non-partner sexual violence. Geneva: World Health Organization. www.who.int/reproductivehealth[4].

World Health Organization, (2015). Violence against women; intimate partner violence and sexual violence. Geneva: World Health Organization. https://www.who.int/ news-room/ fact-sheets/detail/violence-against-women.

---

4. http://www.who.int/reproductivehealth

World Health Organization, (2018). Global Fact Sheet. Violence Against Women: Prevalence Estimates[5]

Yon[6], Y. & Mikton[7], C.R. & Gassoumis[8], Z.D. & Wilber[9], K.H. (2017). Elder abuse prevalence in community settings: a systematic review and meta-analysis, Lancet Global Health, Vol. 5/2, DOI: https://doi.org/10.1016/S2214-109X(17)30006-2

---

5. https://apps.who.int/iris/rest/bitstreams/1349966/retrieve

6. https://pubmed.ncbi.nlm.nih.gov/?term=Yon+Y&cauthor_id=28104184

7. https://pubmed.ncbi.nlm.nih.gov/?term=Mikton+CR&cauthor_id=28104184

8. https://pubmed.ncbi.nlm.nih.gov/?term=Gassoumis+ZD&cauthor_id=28104184

9. https://pubmed.ncbi.nlm.nih.gov/?term=Wilber+KH&cauthor_id=28104184

Appendix

Appendix 1: Types of Domestic Violence Interventions

Table 1: Individual level: Studies that focus on interventions targeted at men or women, irrespective of their belonging to a community, interest group or other collectives		
A1	Economic, income generation	Impact evaluations and systematic reviews of economic interventions and their effects on IPV prevention outcomes. The Intervention itself is typically not designed to prevent IPV, but the study does look into its impact on IPV prevention and risk factors. Examples include microfinance, vocational or job training programmes, and cash transfers.
A2	Social empowerment, skills building, awareness-raising	Interventions focusing on social empowerment through non-economic means target mainly women (particularly from vulnerable groups) and sometimes also men. Interventions include gender sensitisation, transformative programming, awareness-raising about women's rights, access to services, protecting oneself from violence, building soft skills or organisational skills. These interventions can be delivered to groups or one-to-one through home visits for vulnerable individuals. They may focus on health issues, family roles, violence and services available.
A3	Attention to physical or psychological health	Interventions that assist victims by providing physical and psychological health services and work with victimisers when psychological assistance is needed. They are considered if and only if they have a prevention component, or the study deals with their effect on IPV/VAWG prevention outcomes. Physical health includes the treatment of alcohol abuse, but alcohol abuse can also be targeted through other types of interventions.
A4	Bystander interventions	Interventions that organise or promote action taken by a person (or persons) not directly involved as the subject or perpetrator of VAWG to identify, speak out about or seek to engage others in responding to violence. While some forms of bystander action intend to intervene in actual violent incidents, others are designed to challenge the social norms and attitudes that perpetuate violence in the community. They can target men, boys, women or girls.

Relationship and household level: Studies of interventions targeted at i) a couple; ii) members of a couple individually if focused on their interaction; iii) other members of the household identified as key in the prevention of IPV, such as children, in-laws, parents		
B1	Counselling, critical awareness of gender roles	These interventions include workshops and direct counselling for men and women separately or together. They encourage critical awareness of gender roles and norms, promote the position of women, challenge the distribution of resources and allocation of duties between men and women, and address the power relationships between women and others in the community.
B2	Parenting interventions	Interventions targeting parents who have abused or neglected their children, are at risk of doing so or utilise parental roles as a channel for gender role sensitisation. Activities include counselling, role play, media modelling of positive behaviours, structured play, production and delivery of communication materials, etc. They can be delivered through home visits, organised as community-based activities, implemented in a health clinic or other settings.
B3	Curriculum-based activities at school	Interventions delivered at school through formal courses, in-class workshops, or modification at an institutional level of the curricula or educational approaches with an IPV prevention aim.

Source: Picon et al. (2017).

Appendix 2: Characteristics of the DV interventions[1]

Impact Evaluation (IE) Design

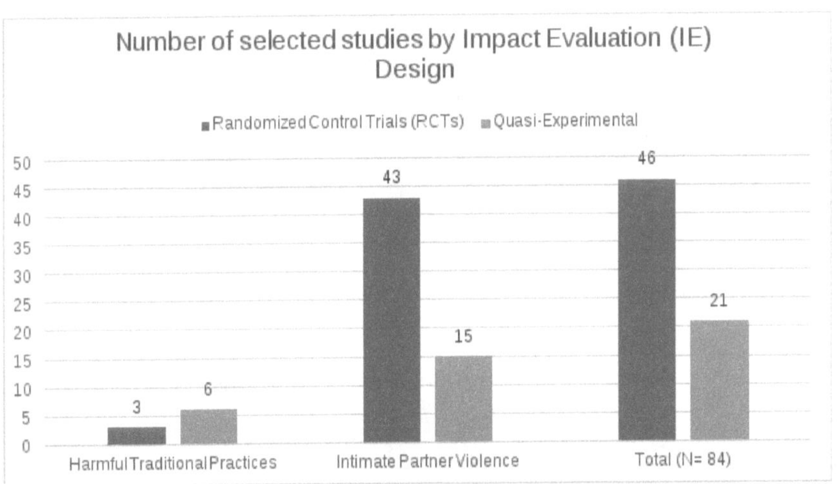

Sample size

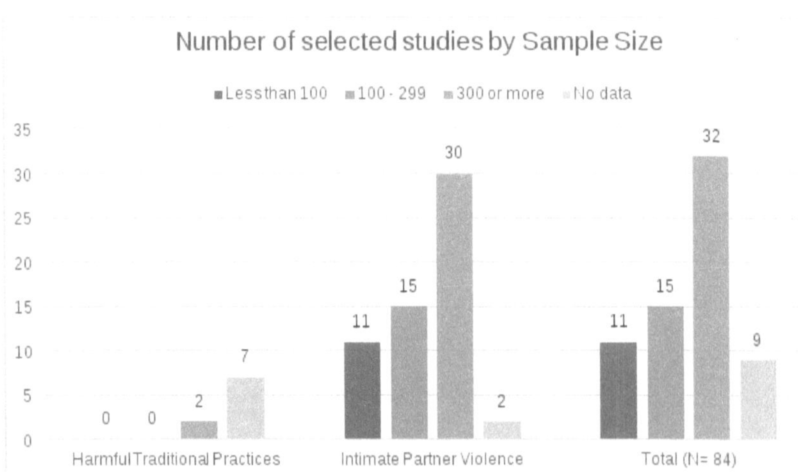

Participants' age

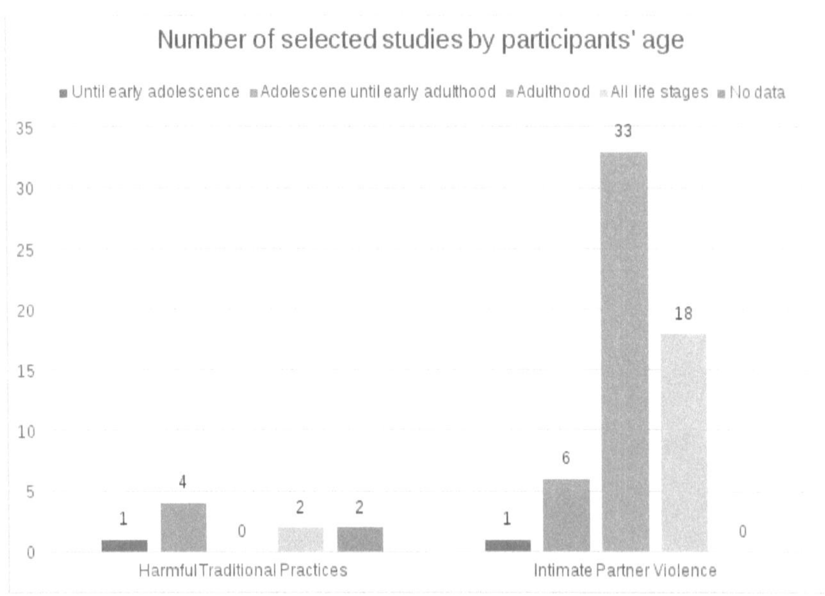

Participants' gender

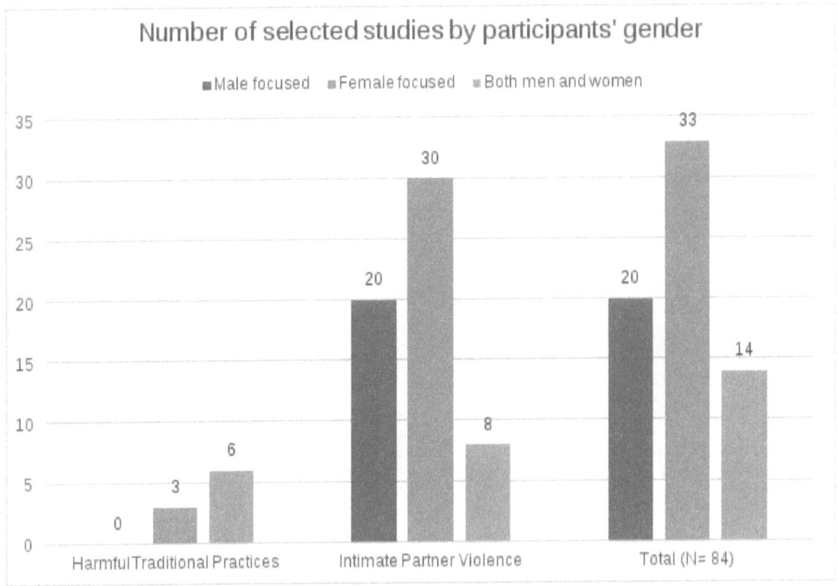

Moment of Intervention (before or after violence occurs)

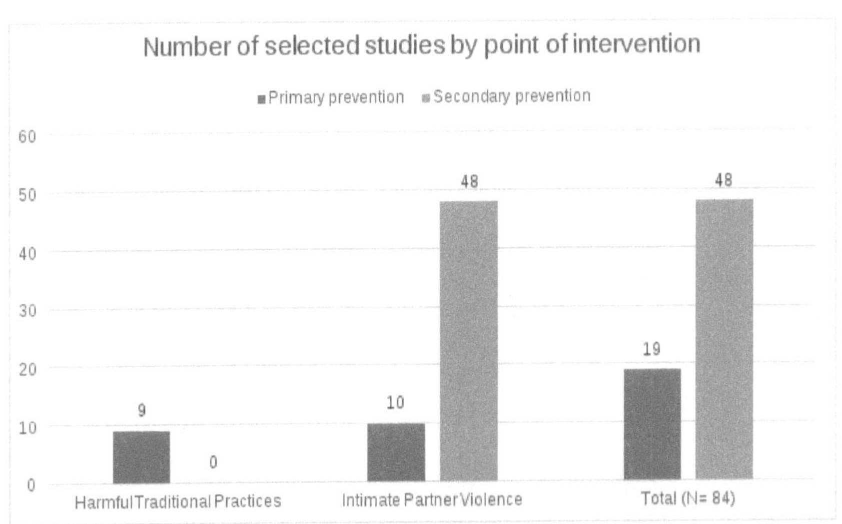

Duration of Intervention

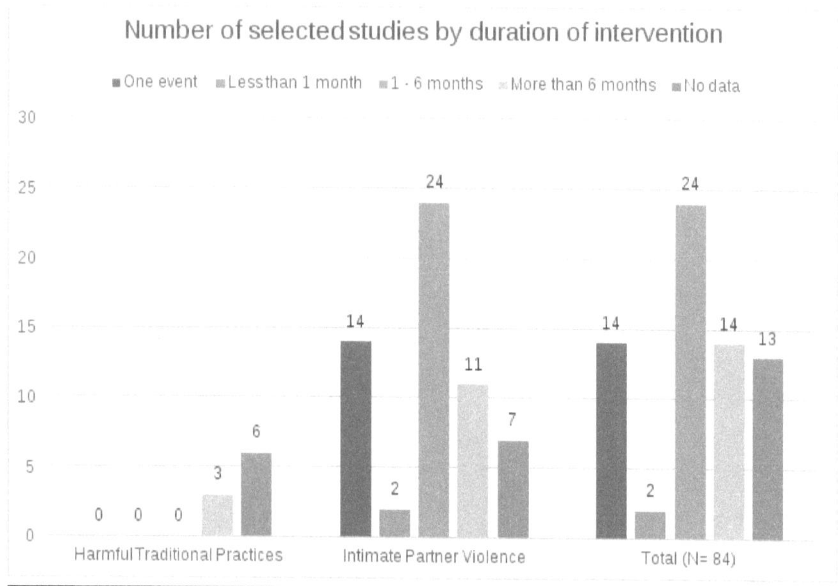

[1] **Source:** Adjusted from Arango et al. (2014). Interventions to prevent or reduce violence against women and girls: A systematic review of reviews. http://dx.doi.org/10.13140/RG.2.1.2545.6168

Don't miss out!

Visit the website below and you can sign up to receive emails whenever Dr. Milos Kankaras publishes a new book. There's no charge and no obligation.

https://books2read.com/r/B-A-LEAZ-CXXZB

BOOKS 2 READ

Connecting independent readers to independent writers.

Also by Dr. Milos Kankaras

A Simple Guide

Lev Vygotsky's Theory of Cognitive Development: A Simple Guide

Gender Equality

Domestic Violence: Effectiveness of Intervention Programs

Standalone

Jean Piaget's Theory of Cognitive Development: A Simple Guide

Watch for more at https://oecd.academia.edu/MilošKankaraš.

About the Author

Dr Miloš Kankaraš is an experienced policy analyst, project manager and author with a rich track record in providing an empirical foundation for evidence-based public policy in international settings. He worked in academia before moving to some of the leading international organisations, where he examined issues ranging from education, skill development, social policy, working conditions, gender equality, quality of life, etc. Miloš published extensively in a variety of policy and research areas. He has an undergraduate degree in Psychology, graduate degrees in educational psychology and international social policy, and a PhD in the area of cross-cultural research.